MW00958635

Dope Cannabis Chronicles

Marijuana Growth Guide for Medicinal and Recreational Use

Dr. Rosemary Spencer

Table of Contents

Introduction

Chapter 1: Introduction to Cannabis Cultivation

Chapter 2: Understanding Cannabis Plants

Chapter 3: Setting Up Your Cannabis Growth Space

Chapter 4: Germination and Seedling Care

Chapter 5: Vegetative Growth and Plant Training Techniques

Chapter 6: Flowering and Bud Development

Chapter 7: Harvesting and Drying Cannabis

Chapter 8: Cannabis Extraction Methods and Products

Chapter 9: Medicinal and Therapeutic Uses of Cannabis

Chapter 10: Responsible Cultivation and Legal Considerations

Conclusion

References

Introduction

Welcome to the world of cannabis, where the green revolution has taken hold, pushing boundaries, challenging perceptions, and transforming lives. In the past few decades, marijuana has emerged from the shadows of prohibition to become a recognized and widely utilized plant for both medicinal and recreational purposes. This revolution has brought about an unprecedented level of curiosity, research, and exploration into the world of cannabis.

The "Dope Cannabis Chronicles" is your definitive guide to understanding and growing cannabis for medicinal and recreational use. Whether you are a novice enthusiast looking to dip your toes into the world of cannabis or an experienced grower seeking to expand your knowledge and refine your techniques, this book will be your trusted companion throughout your journey.

In this guide, we will delve into the rich history of cannabis, exploring its cultural significance, its tangled legal landscape, and its profound impact on individuals and communities across the globe. We will also demystify the science behind marijuana, explaining the intricate chemistry of its compounds and shedding light on the therapeutic potential of cannabinoids and terpenes.

One of this book's core aspects is the art and science of growing marijuana. We will take you step by step through the entire cultivation process, from selecting the right strain and germinating your seeds to nurturing your plants, implementing effective cultivation techniques, and ultimately harvesting high-quality buds. Whether you plan to cultivate indoors or outdoors, we will provide you with the knowledge and insights to optimize your yields and achieve the desired characteristics in your plants.

Understanding the different methods of consumption is essential for any cannabis enthusiast. We will explore various consumption methods, including smoking, vaporizing, edibles, topicals, and more. We will also discuss responsible and safe cannabis use, highlighting the importance of dosage, strain selection, and potential interactions with other substances.

Additionally, this book will navigate the intricate world of cannabis legislation and regulations, helping you stay informed about the legal landscape in different jurisdictions. We will provide an overview of the current legal status of marijuana in various countries and offer insights into emerging trends and potential future developments.

It is crucial to note that the content within "Dope Cannabis Chronicles" is intended for educational and informational purposes only. We strongly encourage you to adhere to the laws and regulations governing cannabis in your region, as they can vary greatly.

The cannabis plant has the power to heal, inspire, and connect us with nature and ourselves. As this green revolution continues to unfold, our mission is to empower you with knowledge, demystify the world of cannabis, and foster responsible and informed use. The journey begins here with "Dope Cannabis Chronicles." So let's embark together on this exploration and unlock the fascinating potential of marijuana for both medicinal and recreational purposes.

Chapter 1: Introduction to Cannabis Cultivation

Cannabis is an incredible plant. Its popularity has been undeniable throughout the ages and continues to make waves today. In this chapter, we will explore the roots of cannabis in ancient civilizations, discover its many varieties and strains that have developed over time, and unravel the complex web of laws surrounding it.

1. A cannabis strain. Source: Forcefield21, CC BY-SA 4.0
<https://creativecommons.org/licenses/by-

The History of Cannabis

Ancient China held a special place for this herb in their traditional medicine rituals, while Taiwan used hemp fibers for textiles. It was even found inside burial sites giving us clues into how important it was to these societies.

The Middle East took note around 2000 BCE praising the medicinal and psychoactive properties of cannabis – they weren't wrong! Clever Egyptians, too, utilized weed in their medical practices, and so did the Greeks and Romans, who loved using beneficial herbs like no other culture before them.

But wait until you hear about Africa, where Rastafarians embraced marijuana within religious ceremonies and throughout cultural activities too! European explorers and traders then brought Cannabis home, which led to increased use all across Europe soon after that journey began centuries ago.

Modern History

Cannabis has had quite a journey in its history. Way back when Europeans were colonizing, and the slave trade was happening, cannabis found its way to America for practical purposes like making rope, sails, and clothes due to its strong fibers. Then people caught on that it could alter their minds, so it became a recreational hit.

But then came the early 1900s with all sorts of misinformation about cannabis spreading fear everywhere - leading countries, including ours here in The United States, to criminalize this plant we now know as marijuana. This birthed The War on Drugs and caused a major uproar across many lands around the globe.

Thankfully, activists and researchers began getting involved during the mid-1900s discovering that cannabis had medical benefits after all, which led them to fight hard against legalization efforts by speaking out about these newfound findings through research studies showing potential therapeutic options available if legalized. And eventually, they got some places to start establishing legit medical pot programs making history.

Varieties and Strains of Cannabis

The main types of cannabis include Cannabis sativa, Cannabis indica, and Cannabis ruderalis. Each one is unique and has different effects on the plant's growth, appearance, and personality.

Let's start with Cannabis sativa. These plants are tall, like skyscrapers, with slender leaves like fingers reaching out for a hug. They take their sweet time to blossom, but when they do, you'll be blessed with an energizing high that gives you focus as sharp as a razor blade - just what you need if you're trying to finish those projects before deadline day!

The next strain, Cannabis indica, stays short but mighty. Its broad leaves spread wide, giving off vibes that make stress disappear faster than Thanos snapped his fingers in Avengers Endgame. Indica strains provide us with a sedative effect perfect for winding down after work or getting some well-needed beauty sleep after hours spent grinding away at the office job all week long.

Lastly, we have the rare gem known as Cannabis ruderalis, hailing from Central Asia, where temperatures dip low enough during winter months. Ruderalis is small yet powerful. Unlike other species, this one can bloom without relying on light cycles making it super useful for breeders looking to create new hybrid versions of classic strains or invent something wild from scratch. So don't expect any ordinary highs here because none come your way whenever these babies hit the scene.

From classics offering legendary psychedelic experiences to modern hybrids mixing traits like ingredients in grandma's secret recipe book, no matter what style of ganja takes your fancy, prepare yourself for an adventure every single time.

Classic Strains

1. **Northern Lights** - Ready to get a little wild? This legendary indica strain has an earthy, sweet aroma that'll transport you into tranquility. It's quick-blooming and resin-rich, so prepare for the body high it packs!

2. **White Widow** – It's another classic hybrid hailing from the Netherlands. Its THC content will really take your breath away, as well as its complex flavor of pine, spice, and everything nice.

3. **OG Kush** - For some serious West Coast vibes, try OG Kush. This popular Indica-dominant hybrid offers a distinctively dank smell and relieves stress and anxiety in no time.

Modern Hybrids

1. **Girl Scout Cookies** - If you're looking to indulge yourself, Girl Scout Cookies is where it's at! GSC has an irresistible

taste featuring sweet earthiness coupled with strong effects thanks to its high THC levels, perfect for relaxation or pain relief after a long day.

2. **Blue Dream** - It takes things up a notch by providing energizing yet calming properties - this sativa-dominant hybrid will give off fruity aromas along with treating depression, stress, and more.

3. **Gorilla Glue** - And if you want something powerful enough to glue you down (pun intended), Gorilla Glue or GG4 is just what you need. Expect sedative effects combined with pungent notes of pine that'll put you into ultimate chill mode while easing chronic pains and helping insomnia too!

Unique Characteristics and Effects

Terpenes and Their Role in Flavor and Aroma:

Terpenes are organic compounds that are like magical essences! From earthy and musky myrcene to zesty limonene and refreshing pinene, these little molecules greatly impact the cannabis experience. Not only do they give each strain its unique flavor profile, but some also believe their influence goes beyond taste, playing an important role in how our bodies react to this herb.

Cannabinoids and Their Effects:

Cannabis has become so much more than just a recreational substance nowadays. It's also home to some pretty awesome chemicals known as cannabinoids. Delta-9-tetrahydrocannabinol (THC) is the one most people are familiar with - its psychoactive effects provide that classic "high" feeling, while cannabidiol (CBD) tends to be a bit more mellow, potentially helping reduce stress and inflammation. But there are other cool ones, too, like cannabinol (CBN), which can bring on major relaxation, and cannabigerol (CBG), which might have brain-protecting powers. No matter which you choose, know that cannabis is here for you!

The Entourage Effect:

What takes things up a notch is something called the entourage effect. When all of those cannabinoids, terpenes, and other compounds work together in harmony, they enhance both therapeutic benefits and overall experience from consuming this plant medicine even more than using one single component alone. That's why experts recommend whole-plant extracts over isolated forms of cannabinoids whenever possible. After all, who doesn't want maximum power?

The Legal Landscape of Cannabis Cultivation

The world of cannabis regulations is always evolving. Today, most countries have their own sets of rules regarding the growth and/or use of cannabis. Here're some notable countries and their cannabis laws:

United States: Federal vs. State Laws

The US government is still playing catch up concerning cannabis laws as they classify it as a Schedule I substance at the federal level. But states have taken charge by allowing medical use or even legalizing recreational use – creating an eclectic patchwork of rules and regulations from coast to coast. Want to grow your own? Make sure you double-check local laws first before planting those seeds.

Canada: Legalization and Regulation

Passing their very own Cannabis Act in 2018, Canada became only the second nation in history (after Uruguay) that had legalized recreational marijuana usage nationwide – making them trendsetters on this front! Homegrown plants are allowed here but stick within limits. Anything more than four plants can land you in hot water, with Health Canada's licensing protocols being strictly enforced for commercial growers. Quality control is no joke either, so rest assured that what goes into your stash will be safe (and delicious).

Cannabis Regulations in Europe

There's something for everyone, from the Netherlands' famous "coffee shops" where you can get your hands on some green to Spain's chill clubs for consumption and cultivation. Even Germany and Italy have their medical marijuana programs, so don't feel left out.

Heading South: Latin America Leads the Way

When it comes to blazing new trails in cannabis policy, Latin American countries are lighting up the way. Uruguay has taken an impressive stance by fully legalizing marijuana, while Mexico is close behind with decriminalization plans in motion. It looks like these regions won't be afraid to make history.

East Meets West: Asia Joins in on the Fun

Asia may not come across as too friendly when it comes to weed, but that doesn't mean they're completely closed off, either. Thailand and South Korea recently jumped on board with medical programs allowing access for those who need it. And if that wasn't enough good news, Australia and New Zealand have also thrown their hats into the ring - even holding referendums about recreational legalization down under (talk about progress).

Cultivation Regulations

Growing cannabis has a few rules you must follow to stay legit. Depending on where you are, regulations can vary from limiting the number of plants or size of your growing area. Canada lets you get away with four for personal use, while down in America, it's based if it's medicinal or recreational use. So make sure to stay informed and cultivate responsibly.

Licensing and Registration: Gaining Access

No way around it - before starting any grow-op mission, you need permission from the proper authorities. In some places, this means tons of documents, background checks, and paying fees. Some even restrict licenses like they're playing Monopoly, so keep an eye out for specific areas that will allow cultivation. Think of them as secret clubs for weed growers!

Quality Control and Testing: Making Sure It Passes Inspection

It's super important that what you're producing is safe and consistent, which is why quality control testing exists. This covers everything from checking pesticides to making sure cannabinoid levels are just right, plus screening for microbes too - don't forget about following those proper practices when cultivating either!

Taxes and Fees: The Unavoidable Reality

Unfortunately, taxes come into play here too. Licensing fees, production/sale taxes, plus property taxes levied against grow facilities all enter the equation at one point or another, but your money goes towards public services like education, healthcare, etc., so there's a silver lining, right?

Security Measures

Protecting your precious plants is essential. That's why laws are in place to keep burglars, sticky fingers, and unauthorized individuals far away from your prized green babies. You'll likely need surveillance cameras, access control systems, and alarm systems to stay safe. And don't forget that you might have to document what you're growing, selling, and who works for you. It's all about maintaining security standards - no exceptions here.

Environmental and Sustainability Considerations

When it comes to the environment, we've to be mindful of our actions when cultivating cannabis. Regulations exist intending to reduce energy consumption and water usage while producing minimal waste and utilizing eco-friendly packaging techniques. Depending on where you're located, some places even offer incentives or certifications for growers who go above and beyond in terms of sustainability efforts.

Medical vs. Recreational Cultivation

Cultivation can come with different sets of rules depending on location and legality status. Medical cannabis often has stricter quality regulations and may require specific strains or products, so proper licenses/registration must be obtained beforehand. Just like any other industry, cannabis culture has its own set of norms requiring us responsible cultivators to stay up-to-date on best practices so success will surely follow suit.

The aspects of cultivating medical cannabis include:

Licensing and Registration: A Necessity for Growing Medical Cannabis

If you want to enter the cannabis business, the first step is obtaining a license or registration. It's not just like getting your standard driver's license. This process requires background checks, security protocols, and financial stability proofing. It's like entering an intense competition! But fear not: it can be done with enough effort and determination.

Choosing Your Strain Wisely: The Key to Successful Cultivation

When cultivating medical marijuana, it pays off (literally) to do your homework when selecting strains. Growers must pick their plants carefully so they produce just the right balance of cannabinoids – meaning those high in CBD for medicinal purposes without inducing any psychoactive effects. In other words? Matchmaking time between plant parents and little ones.

Quality Control: It's a Must for Weed Safety

Weed growers must stay on top of their game, ensuring they adhere to all the rules and regulations. Good Manufacturing Practices (GMP) and approved pesticides are key. Of course, every batch needs thorough testing if it's going to pass muster - safety first! You wouldn't want anyone getting sick or feeling funky after consuming your product, right? Think about it this way: you must ensure that weed is fire before hitting the market. Quality control can help get you there without any trouble.

Standard Operating Procedures

Growers have their playbook for cultivating medical cannabis: the Standard Operating Procedures (SOPs). Think of them as a bible for growing weed - they cover every detail, from watering plants and fertilizing soil all the way down to treating pests. Sticking to these guidelines means you'll always get top-notch ganja. It's all about consistency.

So if you want your bud game strong, make sure SOPs are on lock - because nothing beats quality meds time after time.

Security Measures: Secure Your Precious Buds!

If you're serious about staying in the business of growing weed, it's time to step up your security. Invest in high-tech cameras and access control systems that'll keep everything safe. Ensure alarms are set off if anything fishy is happening with your plants so everyone knows what's happening. Keep meticulous records, too, because these ganja plants need maximum protection.

Stay Informed and Educated: Knowledge Is Power!

As a cannabis connoisseur, staying on top of the ever-evolving industry is essential. To become an ace grower, you've to be informed! Keep up with new cultivation techniques and research medical applications - or even get hands-on experience in studies that are making groundbreaking advancements. Leveraging knowledge is your ticket to standing out amongst all the other green thumbs trying their luck at marijuana growing.

Patient Access and Distribution: A Guide to a Smooth Ride

You've been blessed with some primo medical marijuana - now what? Figuring out the rules and regulations for getting your dope to patients can seem like a mission. But no worries, we got this! Let's explore how easy (and fun) it is to access and distribute medicine safely so everyone can get their daily dose of green goodness.

First things first, you need those connections: dispensaries and doctors who are licensed to carry your product. Having a good understanding of the process will ensure that all parties involved have an effortless experience in terms of compliance. Once that part is handled properly, we must ensure patients get their medication fast. Streamlining orders never looked better!

There are a few things to remember: First and foremost, you must stay up-to-date with the latest industry news and regulations, as well as maintain an excellent level of quality in your work. This will ensure smooth sailing for all involved - no matter how far along we get in this process!

Second, every step forward comes with its own set of responsibilities and more chances to grow professionally and personally. It won't always be easy, but if you keep these tips in mind, you'll be soaring higher than a Marvel superhero before long.

Chapter 2: Understanding Cannabis Plants

Cannabis plants are truly a wonder to behold – and if you want to cultivate them like a pro, then it's essential to understand their chemistry and inner workings. Growers must get familiar with how the plant operates to create an ideal environment for optimal growth, develop desired characteristics, and harvest crops when they're at peak potency. We will explore the fascinating world of cannabis by delving into its structure and functions while also looking at some cutting-edge research that has increased our knowledge about these miraculous plants. From cannabinoids and terpenes production right down to every detail - let's break it down so you can have success growing your pot!

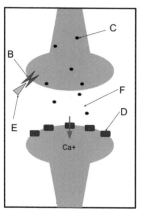 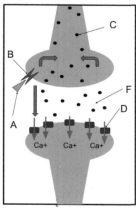

2. *THC connects with CB-1 receptors when marijuana is taken. Dopamine and other neurotransmitters flood the synaptic cleft, causing larger levels of Ca+ to be pumped into the postsynaptic cell. THC then stimulates the reward system in the brain by acting through cannabinoid receptors.*
A) THC / B) CB-1 Receptor / C) Neurotransmitters / D) Postsynaptic Receptors / E) Cannabinoid. Source: Emma guernsey, CC

Anatomy of a Cannabis Plant

1. Leaves

Structure and Appearance

Cannabis leaves are like an exclusive, tropical soiree with leaflets that radiate from a central point. Typically, they come in sets of 5 to 9 leaves but can mix it up depending on their genes and the environment's vibes. These leaflets have a sharp edge lance shape with bold middle veins donning chlorophyll's signature green hue - all thanks to this noteworthy pigment responsible for photosynthesis.

Functional Photosynthesis

These green powerhouses live for photosynthesis. Think of it as magical chemistry, where light energy transforms into glucose (chemical energy). This process goes on inside tiny cells called chloroplasts, which contain chlorophyll plus other pigments helping to convert carbon dioxide and water into oxygen and glucose.

Meaningful Plant Health and Identification

It is said that "leaves never lie" when showing signs of disease/stress or lack of nutrients - cannabis plants stand apart due to their unique leaf structure, making them easily recognizable among other greens!

2. Stems

Structure and Composition

Cannabis stems have three main components: the epidermis, cortex, and vascular cylinder. The epidermis acts as a guard to protect the stem from harm, while within the cortex are cells called collenchyma and parenchyma which give structure and store nutrients. Then there's that star player –the vascular cylinder containing the xylem and phloem responsible for transporting water, vital minerals, and sugars around the plant.

Function in Support and Nutrient Transport

Cannabis stems provide much-needed support keeping plants upright and strong, but they also act like highways carrying all kinds of goodies throughout the plant body, including water via the xylem, minerals through roots to thirsty leaves, and the phloem is on sugar duty, taking photosynthesis produced sweetness everywhere else it needs to go. In other words, these hardworking stems are truly a cheering squad for plants everywhere!

3. Flowers

Structure and Features

Cannabis plants are dioecious, meaning they have two different sexes: male and female. But sometimes, these guys can get wild with hermaphroditic flowers containing both reproductive organs. Let's break it down!

- When we talk about the female, their blossoms feature pistils and calyxes as stars of the show. The pistil is like a diva strutting around with its stigma (the sticky piece) connecting to the style (the support system), leading to an ovary where all kinds of magic happen in those ovules, which turn into seeds if fertilized. Meanwhile, calyces guard the delicate parts within the flower petals.

- Male flowers take center stage, with stamens radiating out from there. The filaments housing anthers at the top generate pollen grains with sperm cells ready for action.

Pollination and Sexual Reproduction

Picture this: an epic cannabis love story where procreation is the main event. Like other plants, the male flowers send their pollen off to meet up with their female flower counterpart - with a little help from Mother Nature's windy ways or some buzzing insect friends. This precious pollen lands on her stigma and starts a fertilization process ending in those cannabis seeds you love.

Significance in Cannabinoid and Terpene Production

These two superstar compounds are what make our favorite plant so special - they're the ingredients responsible for all of cannabis' wild effects, medicinal properties, and out-of-this-world sensory experiences! You can find them mostly hanging inside tiny trichomes (tiny "hairs") covering leaves and buds. These secretory cells create THC, CBD, myrcene, and limonene.

Cannabinoids and Terpenes

It's time to get nerdy about these awesome chemicals found in marijuana plants. Think of cannabinoids as chemical "keys" that interact with our body's endocannabinoid system like no other compound can - unlocking all sorts of amazing therapeutic benefits along the way. When combined with terpenes (the fragrant oils also produced by trichomes), it creates one powerful combo full of flavorful aromas too delicious not to indulge in.

1. Cannabinoids

Definition and Importance

These chemical compounds found in cannabis plants have an amazing talent. They can interact with our body's endocannabinoid system (ECS) to influence how it functions and keep everything running smoothly.

So what is this ECS? It's like a conductor leading our physiological orchestra - made up of receptors, enzymes that create and break down endocannabinoids (cannabinoids naturally produced by our bodies), and phytocannabinoids from plants, which mimic or change these effects.

These powerful phytocannabinoids are responsible for some incredible things - they can alter how you feel physically, mentally, and emotionally. Now, that's something worth trying.

Major Cannabinoids

Cannabis is home to some seriously rad cannabinoids; we're stoked to tell you about them! Let's start with the most researched ones:

- **THC (tetrahydrocannabinol):** This compound gives off a euphoric high, making using marijuana so much fun. But don't forget its therapeutic purposes, either. It helps reduce pain, inflammation, and nausea too.

- **CBD (cannabidiol):** It doesn't produce a psychotropic effect like THC, but it still has major benefits for your body. It can be used as an anti-inflammatory agent or to relieve anxiety without feeling hazy afterward. And if you've had too much THC? No problem. CBD will help balance out any negative side effects like paranoia or jitters.

- **CBN (cannabinol):** It may not have as many fans in the cannabis community as our previous two superstars - but this cannabinoid has plenty of potential when it comes to helping people get their sleep on track. Plus, researchers are studying other applications, such as managing pain and reducing inflammation levels even further!

All these little compounds combine to make one powerful plant medicine that could revolutionize healthcare forever. So let's keep exploring its possibilities.

Medical Applications and Therapeutic Effects

It's no secret that cannabinoids like THC and CBD have been around for years, providing people with relief from pain, inflammation, mental health issues, and so much more. But did you know these all-natural compounds can also protect your brain from damage? It's time to say goodbye to chronic pain management and neuroprotection worries – because cannabis is here!

Let's break down the benefits of cannabinoids one at a time:

- **Pain relief**: With their combined forces of THC and CBD working together as an elite team against nerve pain and swelling symptoms associated with cancer treatment. They won't let any ache stand in their way.

- **Inflammation Fighters:** Your immune system will calm down quickly, thanks to the anti-inflammatory powers of cannabinoids, which can help alleviate joint pains or tummy troubles caused by autoimmune conditions such as multiple sclerosis.

- **Brain Protectors:** Cannabis offers some serious cognitive defense, thanks to its cannabinoid benefit - protecting your brain from diseases like Alzheimer's, Parkinson's, etc., while simultaneously helping reduce anxiety levels related disorders.

- **Mental Makeover Magic:** Mental health struggles don't stand a chance when faced with cannabinoids, either. Research has shown promise in aiding those suffering from depression and PTSD, and schizophrenia.

So if you're looking for natural ways to improve overall well-being (without worrying about side effects), then cannabis could be just what you need!

2. Terpenes

Terpenes are the organic compounds that give plants, including our beloved cannabis buds, their unique aroma and taste. But even more than just creating a flavor profile for your strain of choice - terpenes also work to protect against pests and diseases. Plus, they join forces with cannabinoids in marijuana to magnify their therapeutic properties through something called "the entourage effect." That's right. Terpenes team up with CBDs to bring us an extra layer of healing benefits of cannabis.

Some Cool Terpenes Found in Cannabis

Here are a few terpenes that you'll often find in cannabis plants:

- **Myrcene**: Not only is this magical molecule the most abundant terpene in cannabis strains, but it also packs a powerful punch with its intense earthy-musky aroma. It's not just for show, either. Studies suggest that myrcene can reduce inflammation, relieve pain, and even works as a sedative. If you want to chill out after a long day or amp up your wellness routine, look no further than this terpene.

- **Limonene**: This terpene will give you a boost like no other when it comes to anxiety relief, mood enhancement, and immunity strengthening.

- **Caryophyllene**: Caryophyllene has a unique flavor profile that encourages communication between CB2 receptors in the body, which helps combat inflammation, soothe pain, and protect neurons.

- **Pinene**: Pinene-infused cannabis strains are known to aid breathing issues, reduce inflammation, and improve memory capabilities - all whilst making you feel one with Mother Nature herself.

- **Linalool**: It offers relaxation, thanks to its lavender scent that calms even the most anxious among us while combating depression symptoms at the same time.

The Aroma, Flavor, and Healing Powers of Terpenes

Terpenes are the flavor magicians of cannabis, giving each strain its own unique experience. But their power doesn't end there! These aromatic warriors team up with cannabinoids to supercharge the therapeutic effects of marijuana. Together they form an unstoppable duo for health and wellness.

Scientists are still uncovering what terpenes can do. Early studies show promise in relieving pain, reducing inflammation, and calming nerves to regulate moods. Yet we need more research to understand how these molecules work together with cannabinoids and our bodies. That's why it's time for us to dig deeper into this dynamic duet so we can take full advantage of nature's healing powers!

The Life Cycle of Cannabis Plants

1. Germinating a Cannabis Plant: A Step-by-Step Guide

If you want to grow your cannabis, the germination stage is where it all begins. To kick off your cultivation journey on the right foot, understanding how this process works - and what conditions are needed for success - is paramount.

Process and Optimal Conditions

Germination occurs when water penetrates the outer layer of the seed and brings about its transformation into a sprout. This leads to root development and shoot emergence, with a set of leaves soon following suit. Generally speaking, temperatures between 68°F (20°C) and 77°F (25°C), adequate moisture levels in the growing medium, and proper oxygenation will aid in successful germination efforts.

Seed Selection and Storage

Before you get started, be sure to select top-notch seeds. Brown or dark gray seeds with firm shells are best avoided. Pale green or visibly damaged ones may have reduced rates of growth potential. For optimal storage, keep them somewhere cool, dark, and dry. An airtight container should do just fine, but whatever you do, avoid extreme temperature fluctuations or high humidity that could potentially alter their potency over time.

2. Vegetative Growth Stage

Characteristics and Duration

The vegetative growth stage is a period of rapid development for leaves, stems, and roots. It's all about growing tall and establishing a strong root system - the length varies depending on the strain, environment conditions, or desired plant size, but it usually takes 4-8 weeks in indoor growth.

Optimal Conditions for Vegetative Development

For optimal vegetative growth, set your light timer: 18-24 hours per day with full spectrum grow lights will do the trick! The temperature should be kept between 70-85°F (21-29°C) while humidity levels should remain steady at 40%-60%.

Nutrition and Water Management

Nutrient intake is especially important during this stage - nitrogen helps promote healthy leaf/stem growth, so make sure it's incorporated into your fertilizer mix. When it comes to watering, don't go overboard. Wait until the top inch of soil feels dry before giving plants their next drink. Too much water results in root rot and other issues, while under-watering can lead to stunted development. Nobody wants that!

3. Flowering

Flowering Stage

When the sun sets, it's time for cannabis plants to begin their transition into the reproductive phase. As day turns to night and darkness envelops them, an incredible transformation occurs, whereby buds develop with a high concentration of cannabinoids and terpenes.

Identifying Male and Female Plants

It's essential to differentiate male from female plants to protect your harvest quality from unwanted pollination. Males can be recognized by pollen sacs near their leaf nodes, while females will have small hairs called pistils.

Optimal Growing Conditions for Flowering Cannabis

Light: 12/12 cycle of light and dark is essential to get your plants popping. That's twelve hours of sunshine followed by an equal amount of darkness.

Temperature: Keep your grow room at a cozy 65-80°F (18-27°C) so those buds can flourish! Cooler nighttime temps might even help with color and terpene production in some strains.

Humidity: As the flowers develop, gradually reduce relative humidity levels to 40-50%, as too much moisture could lead to mold or bud rot.

4. Harvest

Determining the Optimal Harvest Time

It's time to get your green thumb on and figure out when to harvest cannabis! To ensure the best cannabinoid and terpenes profile, it all comes down to examining trichomes. As plants mature, these tiny crystal-like structures transition from clear to milky, then amber.

Reap your rewards when most of them are milky but with some amber ones in there too. That balance is key for maximum potency and flavor! If you're not sure about the trichomes yet, another way is looking at pistils: once they've changed color from white to orange or brown and curled inwardly, it may be a sign that harvest time has returned.

Harvesting Techniques

Whether you're an amateur gardener or an experienced cultivator, getting the timing right can make all the difference for those sweet buds. There are two main ways of harvesting:

- **Wet trimming**- The fan leaves and sugar leaves around buds are removed while the plant is still fresh. It tends to be simpler since the leaves stay stiffer.

- **Dry trimming**- The entire plant/large branches are hung up first before trimming. It helps maintain aroma as the drying process moves slower, so more control over the quality outcome is possible here too.

Whichever method is chosen, though, remember gentleness must reign during handling. Don't go roughhousing those delicate trichomes! Afterward, put them through proper drying and curing processes with 5-15 days set aside for the former and 2 weeks to several months dedicated towards the latter, depending on the results desired.

Chapter 3: Setting Up Your Cannabis Growth Space

The world of cannabis cultivation requires you to know the best growth practices. Whether you're growing it just for your stash or to spread the love around, there are two options at hand: indoor or outdoor. It's up to you which direction you choose—the choice is yours. In this chapter, we'll explore all aspects of each option so that regardless of your path, both will have their highs and lows.

3.   Cannabis fields in Ketama, Morroco. Source: GuHKS, CC BY-SA 4.0

Indoor Cultivation

Pros

- **Temperature, humidity, and light control**: Nail down that perfect paradise for your cannabis crops by having complete control over temperature, humidity, and light levels. This gives them optimal conditions necessary for their health while maximizing those yields.

- **Year-round harvest party**: No more waiting around on unpredictable weather patterns! Enjoy multiple harvests throughout all seasons when you step into the world of indoor cultivation with a never-ending supply guaranteed year-round – it's time to invite everyone over for some green goodness and fun times ahead.

- **Reduced risk of pests and diseases**: Keep pesky pests or diseases at bay by keeping things sterile inside, so they won't have a chance at wreaking havoc on everything you've worked hard towards achieving.

- **Greater yield potential**: You can now fine-tune every aspect within this controlled environment, which will unlock their full potential allowing them to reach great heights like training and pruning techniques.

Cons

- **High initial investment:** Setting up an indoor grow space can come with a hefty price tag due to the need for specialized gear like lighting fixtures, air ventilation systems, and climate control devices. Even if you have deep pockets, it's way pricier than just throwing some seeds in the dirt outside!

- **High energy consumption**: Once you've got everything going, there's also an increased demand for energy as most indoor growing requires artificial lighting (think of all those glowing bulbs), plus temperature/humidity control that also needs power.

- **Demanding maintenance**: Achieving optimal growing conditions can be tricky, too, so don't expect "set-and-forget" when cultivating inside – constant monitoring and adjustments are required if you want your buds to reach their full potential. In short?

Growing cannabis indoors is not a walk in the park. But if done right, it pays off.

Outdoor Cultivation

Pros

- **Saves your dough**: Setting up an outdoor marijuana garden is far more cost-effective than indoor, as you don't have to invest in all the fancy equipment. Plus, Mother Nature has got your back with free sun and fresh air!

- **Eco-friendly**: With outdoor growing, you're not wasting electricity on lighting systems like indoors, saving you money and positively impacting our planet.

- **Let that sun shine down**: Natural sunlight makes plants stronger and more potent than those grown under artificial light. Plus, it just feels better knowing that nature's golden rays nourished your buds.

Cons

- **Environmental factors:** Outdoor marijuana cultivation is a high-stakes game of chance with Mother Nature, including unpredictable weather changes, pests, and diseases. These elements can be harder to monitor and may hurt your plants' health and yield.

- **Seasonal growing limitations**: Cannabis requires certain light cycles for it to progress through its various growth stages - so outdoor weed farming is usually only possible during the growing season, which differs depending on where you are located.

- **Lack of control over conditions**: When cultivating cannabis outdoors, you don't have as much control over the environment compared to indoor farming, making it more difficult to create the ideal conditions needed for a successful harvest.

At the end of the day, both indoor and outdoor cannabis gardening come with their unique benefits and drawbacks - requiring growers like yourself to weigh these factors carefully before deciding what best fits their preferences, budget, and available resources. Ultimately though, there's no one right answer when choosing between indoor or outdoor growing. Just whatever will give you joy in reaping your rewards as a dope grower!

Factors to Consider When Choosing a Grow Space

When it comes to setting up your cannabis grow space, the decision of whether you should go outdoors or indoors is a big one. You have to make sure you get what's best for you and have an awesome experience growing weed. Keep these key points in mind before taking the plunge:

1. Location

It pays off to do some research beforehand on where's good for you because there are a few things that could hold you back from having an epic harvest season if not taken into consideration:

- **Legalities:** First and foremost, check out what laws apply in your area, if it's even legal at all! There might also be restrictions on how many plants you can keep or how far away they have to stay from schools and parks etc. So don't skip this step!

- **Privacy:** Weed has got a pretty dank odor during flowering, which means keeping nosey neighbors away is essential. Opt for inside grows with dedicated rooms/tents that won't mess with the rest of your living space, or find somewhere outside that's not too obvious (like maybe behind trees).

- **Security:** Don't let anyone ruin your hard work by stealing or vandalizing your plants. Use fences and barriers around outdoor spaces, while indoor ones need proper locks/security systems installed when no one's around watching them.

2. Space Availability

The amount of space you have for your cannabis grow will make a big difference in whether you go with indoor or outdoor cultivation.

Indoor Growing: If you're cultivating cannabis indoors, consider the size of your space and ensure it will accommodate the number of plants you want and all necessary equipment. Grow lights, ventilation systems - don't forget that these plants can get tall. Make sure there's enough headroom too.

Outdoor Cultivation: Whether you've got a sprawling backyard or a cozy balcony, outdoor growing is an awesome way to flex your green thumb. The size of your grow area will determine how creative and ambitious you can be. If it's large and open, why not try trellising or hydroponics? Smaller spaces mean smaller containers - but that doesn't have to limit you either. Get artsy with vertical gardening for maximum impact in minimal places.

3. Budget

The money you'll be spending on your cannabis cultivation matters. Whether it's indoors or outdoors, each option comes with its financial pros and cons.

Indoor Growing: If you don't want to feel like a cheapskate, indoor growing is your best bet. It can set you back big time since fancy necessities such as grow lights, climate control systems, and ventilation require an ongoing stream of cash. Plus, those electricity bills will soon add up!

Outdoor Growing: You might think outdoor growing is more wallet-friendly than its indoor counterpart, but that is not always the case. To keep things running smoothly outside, you may need to make some soil adjustments and stock up on nutrients plus pest prevention products - all costing you dough in the long run. So keep an eye out for those pesky costs if opting for this route! Bottom line? Weighing both options against your budget should help steer you right when it comes to choosing between indoors or outdoors.

4. Time Commitment

Cultivating marijuana takes effort, but don't worry – you can do it successfully. The amount of energy and thought that goes into your project will help determine whether growing indoors or outside is right for you.

Going Indoor: If indoor cultivation is your game plan, be ready to become their caregiver. Plants bred in an indoor environment need continuous attention as conditions are constantly monitored and tweaked to make sure they're perfect for growth. From keeping track of humidity levels to managing light cycles like a pro - being prepared means being successful!

Growing Outside: But if Mother Nature has your back, outdoor cultivating may be just what's needed. You still have to put in some time, but many elements come from nature itself - sunshine providing natural warmth plus air loaded with nutrients all mean quicker growth times than traditional methods would allow! Of course, there can always be unexpected problems like pests or diseases which could ruin everything, so keep watchful eyes on those green babies at all times!

So before starting any pot-planting adventure, consider how much free time you can give up first - because no matter where it's done (indoors or out), dedication will ultimately lead down the road towards success!

Tips for Growing Killer Cannabis Plants

When it comes to growing some fire cannabis plants, creating the right environment is key. Whether you're cultivating your indoor grow-op or rolling up your sleeves and getting dirty in a backyard garden, essential factors should be considered for a successful harvest. Let's take a closer look:

1. Light

Growers need to be savvy when it comes to lighting their indoor gardens - after all, they have to emulate the sun's spectrum and intensity! Luckily, there are a few options available for the clever cultivator.

- **HID (High-Intensity Discharge):** These bad boys hit like major powerhouses and can yield some serious results. Just watch out because they eat up electricity and get hot AF! We're talking Metal Halide (MH) lamps and High-Pressure Sodium (HPS) here.

- **LEDs:** The cool kids of energy efficiency and low heat output with customizable spectrums. Although slightly pricier than other options, LED lights are worth every penny spent in the long run.

- **CFLs (Compact Fluorescent Light):** For those looking for an eco-friendly option that won't burn through your wallet or your plants - look no further than CFLs! They don't get too hot, so if you've got some big-time growth going on, this probably won't cut it.

- **Light cycles:** When it comes down to timing, we know our green friends have got to follow suit just like us humans – during the vegetative stage, 18 hours light and 6 hours dark is what you want, but come the flowering season, it's 12/12.

- **Placement and height:** Last but not least, make sure you keep an eye on how far away from your lamps the plants stay; otherwise, scorched leaves. Too close means a one-way ticket straight to getting burnt.

2. Ventilation Is Essential

Proper airflow in your grow space is critical for keeping things healthy and avoiding problems like mold, mildew, and disappointment. Plus, it's great for the plants!

- **Why fresh air matters**: A nice breeze regulates temperature and humidity and supplies the carbon dioxide that plants need to photosynthesize. So give them some love - just like a gentle coastal wind blowing through their leaves!

- **Different types of ventilation:** You have two main choices: passive systems that let air flow naturally or active setups with fans and vents to control movement. Indoor growers usually go with an active approach, while outdoor ones can rely on Mother Nature.

- **The magic of exhaust fans and intake vents:** When you're growing indoors, exhaust fans are your friends. They suck out hot, stuffy air while intake vents bring in sweet relief from the fresh cool, oxygen-rich air.

- **Keep that stinky smell away**: During flowering time, when your buds start giving off their unique pungency aroma, don't panic – pair up exhaust fans with carbon filters so no one has to do any bloodhound sniffing around town.

3. **Temperature Control: Keeping It Cool**

When it comes to cannabis plants, controlling the temperature is essential for their growth and health. To ensure they stay just right, here are some handy tips you can use in your growing space - indoors or out!

- **Heat and AC:** If you're going with indoor cultivation, heaters and air conditioners help regulate temperatures according to what's happening outside. Think of them like a thermostat for your green babies!

- **Insulation:** Wrapping up your grow room so that nothing gets too hot or cold gives an extra layer of protection against any sudden weather changes. Plus, you'll save energy while doing so.

- **Shade cloth (outdoor):** For outdoor growers looking to protect their crops from scorching summer days, shade cloths are like capes made for superheroes...or at least super plants! They provide shelter from the sun's rays without blocking out vital light.

4. Humidity Control – Staying Balanced

Keeping humidity levels balanced is also key when growing cannabis. During the vegetative stage, 40%-70% relative humidity works best, whereas, during flowering, this should be lowered slightly (40%–50%). So how do we achieve this? Here are a few ideas:

- **Humidifiers and dehumidifiers**: These nifty gadgets help maintain optimal moisture levels by adding/reducing water vapor in the air as needed - perfect if conditions shift suddenly outdoors.

- **Ventilation systems**: Ensuring good airflow will control humidity and prevent moldy mildew parties from popping up where they shouldn't be. So get those fans humming away!

Necessary Gear for Epic Cannabis Cultivation

Growing weed is like having a superpower; the right tools can help you unleash your inner superhero. Whether you're growing indoors or out, here's what you need to take your cannabis garden to greater heights:

- **Lights (for indoor):** For plants that live inside, artificial illumination will have them thriving. HID lights, LED lamps, and CFLs all offer different benefits in terms of budgeting and efficiency - pick whichever suits your needs best!

- **Ventilation system:** Your green babies need fresh air chock full of oxygen if they're going to be at their peak performance level. Indoor growers should consider exhaust fans plus intake vents for optimal airflow. Outdoor growers just got to make sure there's some wind action happening while also using fences or screens when necessary from strong gusts.

- **Temperature and humidity control:** Keep it comfortable for healthy growth by monitoring temperature and humidity levels accordingly. If indoors, then think of heaters/air conditioning units plus humidifiers/dehumidifiers. What about the outdoors? Shade cloths and potentially an off-the-hook greenhouse are key players here!

- **Home sweet home:** Give them something comfy to call home with options ranging from plastic pots to trendy fabric ones, even snazzy raised beds as well - don't forget drainage holes, though, so no waterlogging happens.

- **Prepare your soil:** You have to be choosy when it comes to picking out a growing medium for your buds! Whether you go classic with soil or try something new (think coco coir or perlite/vermiculite/rock wool), find one that fits both your style and environment.

- **Feed them up**: Like us humans, marijuana plants have nutritional needs, too – nitrogen, phosphorus, and potassium, plus sidekicks such as calcium, magnesium, and iron should all be on the menu here. Plenty of nutrient solutions are made specifically for cannabis, so follow those directions closely if you want to keep these babes happy and healthy!

- **Hydrate**: Watering is an essential part of keeping your crop alive and kicking – whether by hand watering or using a drip irrigation system will depend on what works best in your setup, but always aim for the perfect balance between overhydrating and under-watering, you know? It might sound basic but trust us; this step can't be skipped if you want to see results from your garden come harvest season.

- **Get testing (pH and TDS/EC Meters):** Think of these meters as personal physicians checking up on your plants regularly - making sure the pH levels plus total dissolved solids (TDS) / electrical conductivity (EC) stay at optimal levels helps ensure proper nutrient absorption which is vital to the health of your buds.

- **Keep out those pesky pests and diseases**: Nobody wants unexpected guests to be uninvited to make things difficult for your green beauties, right? Nip any signs of pests and diseases early with organic or chemical pest control products like insecticides and fungicides to keep them away for good.

Chapter 4: Germination and Seedling Care

Germination and seedling care are essential for a successful cannabis cultivation experience. Laying the groundwork for healthy plants and getting optimal yields is made possible with proper attention to these early stages of growth. Here's how you can do it right!

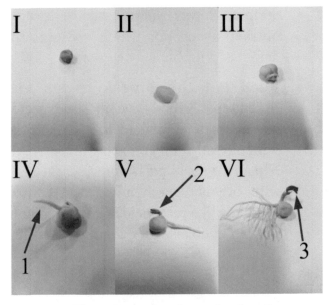

4. *The process of seed germination. Source: Noahjgagne, CC BY-SA 4.0*

Methods: Sowing the Seeds of Success

Getting your crops off the ground starts with germination – that is when the water activates enzymes and hormones inside the seed, which cause its protective shell to crack open. This leads to the development of roots (called radicles) that anchor themselves into the growing medium, followed by shoots pushing upwards through the soil before producing cotyledons (the first set of leaves).

1. Paper Towel Method

Materials: Gather Your Supplies

To get started, you need the following items handy:

- Cannabis seeds
- Two plates/plastic bags
- Moistened paper towels (not drenched!)
- Distilled water
- Tweezers

Instructions:

1. Moisten two pieces of paper towel using distilled H2O until damp but not soggy - one piece goes on a plate/bag while the other sits aside for later.

2. Using those trusty tweezers mentioned earlier - carefully space out each seed evenly across the first sheet of a damp towel.

3. Place the second wetted sheet over the top and seal the edges by placing the second plate/bag atop, creating a dome effect (or partially sealed plastic bag).

4. Store in a warm dark area at an optimal temperature range between 68°F - 77°F (20°C - 25°C). Keep daily tabs on moisture levels plus any signs of germination egressing from within tiny little shell(s). If drying occurs, add a light spritz of water as needed.

Time to Transplant

After radicle emergence (~ 0.5 inches), it's time to transplant into desired soil medium, ensuring not to touch the radicle directly with bare hands as this is indeed ultra-delicate stuff. Use sterilized tweezers and grip with care when moving seedlings safely into their new home, making sure the root faces downwards before lightly covering the surface with a thin layer of soil, then mist overhead generously and place under a gentle lighting source monitoring progress regularly thereafter.

2. Water Germination Method

You've got the seeds; now it's time to get them ready for some serious growing. Here's what you need:

- Cannabis seeds
- A glass or jar
- Distilled H2O
- Tweezers (or a steady hand!)

Instructions:

1. Prepare your container with distilled water so that it is deep enough to submerge all of your seeds.

2. Grip each seed with tweezers and place it into the water one by one - be careful not to drop any!

3. Place in a warm, dark environment between 68°F and 77°F (20-25°C).

4. Check daily – after around 24-48 hours, your little nuggets should start sinking, and emerging radicles will begin appearing. If they haven't sunken yet, give them a gentle stir to help them out.

Monitoring and Transplanting Time

Once everything has made its way down below the surface and healthy-looking rootlets have peeked their heads out from underneath, you're ready for transplantation day! Using clean tweezers once again, carefully remove each germinated seed from the liquid gold bathtub and lay them gently on top of pre-moistened soil/medium - make sure those roots are facing downwards, as this is super important for successful growth later on. Top off with another light layer of the medium before misting over everything lightly, then placing it under an appropriate light source.

3. Germination Kits

Germinating cannabis seeds doesn't have to be complex. Germination kits provide a simple solution for growing your plants, offering several advantages:

- Pre-moistened media designed for optimal sprouting
- Tightly regulated humidity and temperature levels
- Decreased risk of contamination or disease
- Easier transplantation into larger containers later on.

Popular germination kit options include:

- Rapid Rooter Starter Plugs
- Jiffy Pellets

- Grodan Rockwool Cubes
- Root Riot Starter Cubes

Instructions:

1. Pick the right germination kit based on your preferences, then read through the manufacturer's instructions to prepare it properly.

2. Using tweezers, carefully insert the cannabis seed into the pre-moistened medium provided in each setup - this is key!

3. Place everything in a warm dark spot where temperatures are maintained between 20-25°C (68-77°F).

4. Keep an eye out daily, as most strains will begin to pop up within 24–72 hours.

5. Monitor moisture levels often and water accordingly as needed per manufacturers' guidelines.

4. Direct Soil Germination

For direct soil germination, you'll need the following:

- Cannabis seeds
- High-quality potting soil or growing medium

- Containers with drainage holes
- Distilled water

Instructions:

1. Fill your containers up to 1-2 inches (2.5-5 cm) from the top with the chosen growing medium, and lightly moisten them with distilled water - not saturated!

2. Use tweezers to carefully place each cannabis seed 0.25-0.5 inches (0.6-1.3 cm) down into the soil and cover them over with a thin layer of dirt again, misting on top afterward if needed for extra moisture retention in between checking for growth daily!

3. Cover everything up tightly using either a humidity dome or some plastic wrap - then set aside in a warm, dark spot around 68–77°F (20–25°C).

4. Once sprouts have emerged after about three days up until ten days later, take off any covering used.

Transplanting

Move the plants under a gentle light source like an LED lamp while monitoring progress through healthy leaf development, such as cotyledons and true leaves, alongside adequate hydration levels of dampness but not overly wet areas!

As the seedlings develop, it's time to think about transplanting them into larger pots. Keep a close eye on their progress. If you notice roots popping out of the drainage holes or slow growth, that likely means they need more space soonest possible!

When you're ready to move them up in size, carefully take each one out of its current pot and place it in a new container with an appropriate soil medium – then keep monitoring and caring for your little ones as they enter the veg and flower stages. Don't forget: those plants are growing fast. So make sure you stay on top of things.

Caring for Cannabis Seedlings: A Must-Know Guide

As any grower knows, cannabis seedlings are incredibly delicate and require specific care to ensure they develop into strong plants. To help you give your babies the best start in life, this guide outlines all the essential aspects of seedling care - from watering and lighting to temperature/humidity control. Think of it as giving your little green sprouts an early edge!

1. Watering

When it comes to maintaining healthy growth in cannabis seedlings, proper watering is key. Not only does water allow vital nutrients to travel through the plant, but it also supports countless metabolic processes within its cells. If you don't get this right, then nutrient deficiencies, root rot, or stunted growth can occur.

Signs of Overwatering and Underwatering

Signs that you're overwatering include yellow leaves, wilting despite moist soil, and slow development. Underwatering symptoms involve dry soil crumbles alongside wilted leaves and drooping/curled foliage with slowed growth rate.

Watering Frequency

It's imperative that when caring for young marijuana plants, you follow these simple steps:

- Check the top 1-2 inches (2.5-5 cm) of soil each time before adding H20 - it should be slightly damp, not saturated.

- Gently hydrate using a spray bottle or fine nozzle on a small can.

- Apply fluid evenly around the base, avoiding stems/leaves.

- Allow minor drying between watering so the roots have a chance to breathe.

2. Lighting

Light Requirements for Seedlings

Cannabis seedlings need a boatload of light to photosynthesize and grow up big and strong. This early stage requires consistent lighting with the right spectrum for vigorous vegetative development - an 18/6 cycle of 18 hours on, 6 hours off. If you're just starting as a budding grower, here are some options for your green thumb:

- Fluorescent Lights (CFLs or T5 tubes): The economical choice that provides cool blue light perfectly suited for seedling growth. They get the job done without breaking the bank - it's no wonder they're so popular among novice growers!

- LED Grow Lights: Super modern LED lights come packed with full-spectrum capabilities, energy efficiency, and longevity like nothing else on this list...but also at quite a high price point compared to other choices. Still worth investing in if you want serious results, though!

- Metal Halide (MH) Lights: MH bulbs channel their magical plant-growing powers through intense blue light spectrums. You just have to ensure you have proper cooling systems set up because they generate heat like nobody's business!

Proper Light Distance and Duration

It's no secret that cannabis cultivation can be a tricky endeavor. But with the right tender loving care, you can get your plants through those crucial early stages and onto bigger and better things! To keep them thriving, stick to an 18/6 light cycle - photosynthesis is essential for growth, but too much of it will only cause undue stress.

Make sure to position lighting sources at appropriate distances away from plants as well. Say 4-6 inches (10-15 cm) for fluorescents and 18-24 inches (45-60 cm) for LEDs and MH lamps.

Watering should also be on point - establish a schedule and stick to it so that seedlings are neither over nor under-hydrated. While there's never been a better time than now to flex your green thumb skillset, remember, when it comes down to growing ganja like a pro, patience is key!

Common Challenges and Solutions

Cultivating cannabis can be incredibly fun and rewarding, but it comes with unique challenges. In this chapter, we'll discuss some common problems growers face - from damping off to nutrient deficiencies and pests and diseases - as well as their solutions so you can ensure a successful harvest!

1. Damping Off: Causes and Symptoms

Damping off is a frustrating issue that affects young seedlings due to soil-borne fungi like Pythium, Rhizoctonia, or Fusarium. These fungi thrive in high humidity conditions with poor air circulation. Symptoms include:

- Failing seedlings
- Root rot/decay
- Yellow leaves
- Slow growth
- Thin water-soaked stems that cause collapse at the base of the plant

Prevention and Treatment Methods

To prevent damping off in your garden:

- Use sterile growing media for drainage purposes.

- Maintain proper temperature/humidity levels (as discussed previously).

- Increase airflow around seedlings using small fans or brushing them daily.

- Avoid overwatering, which can create an ideal environment for fungus growth.

If you think damping off has already attacked your plants, you can:

- Try removing affected ones quickly before it spreads any further

- Apply fungicides such as copper-based solutions or biological control agents like Trichoderma according to directions on the packaging.

- Increase air circulation while decreasing humidity to help rescue the remaining healthy plants too.

2. Nutrient Deficiencies

Identifying Common Deficiencies in Seedlings

When it comes to cannabis seedling health, a lack of essential elements can spell disaster.

Let's break down the common deficiencies that may arise and what they look like:

- **Nitrogen (N):** You'll see yellowing of lower leaves, slow growth, and feeble stems.

- **Phosphorus (P):** Dark green or purple foliage indicates phosphorus deficiency, sluggish growth, and underdeveloped roots.

- **Potassium (K):** The edges of the leaves turn yellowish-brown while curling inward. You might also notice slower-than-usual growth along with weak stems.

- **Calcium (Ca):** Stunted development, distorted leaf shapes, and feeble roots are all signs your plant is lacking calcium!

- **Magnesium (Mg):** Yellow veins on a lighter-colored background with curled-up leaves indicate magnesium deprivation, resulting in weak stem strength too.

Fixing Nutritional Imbalances

Nutrient deficiencies in cannabis seedlings can be tricky to tackle, but by following this step-by-step guide, your plants will thrive again in no time.

- First, identify the specific deficiency by comparing symptoms to known ones. If you're using a pre-mixed nutrient solution, make sure it contains all essential elements and is formulated specifically for cannabis growth.

- Adjust the pH of both your growing medium and nutrient solution– because nutrients won't be absorbed properly if not! The ideal range for soil-grown plants is 6.0 - 7.0, while hydroponic systems should aim to stay between 5.5 - 6 .5 on the pH scale.

- Once that's done, you can apply any necessary supplements according to their instructions. One wrong move here could do more harm than good, so double-check before adding anything!

- Finally, keep tabs on progress over time, adjusting levels as needed until the balance has been restored.

3. Pests and Diseases

These pesky pests and diseases will have your cannabis seedlings looking worse for wear:

- **Spider mites**- The tiny terrors that cause the yellowing of leaves and eventual leaf drop.

- **Aphids** - Sap-suckers that promote curling and distortion of green growth.

- **Fungus gnats** – Their larvae feed on plant roots to create stunted plants.

- **Powdery mildew**- A white powdery fungus leading to yellowing foliage.

Integrated Pest Management (IPM)

Pest management is the key tool for controlling critters without harming the environment or endangering human health. Here are our top tips for preventing potential problems with your green babies:

- Check-in regularly – Inspect your plants frequently so unwelcome visitors don't have a chance to take over.

- Make sure conditions stay optimal – Maintain proper temperature, humidity levels, and air circulation as pathogens thrive in dampness.

- Practice cleanliness– Use sterile growing mediums and sterilized equipment when introducing new additions.

- Employ natural predators– Ladybugs or predatory mites can help keep other bugs in check.

- Get biological control agents involved– Beneficial bacteria or fungi can help combat disease before it takes hold.

- Use low-toxicity pesticides sparingly - Insecticidal soaps, oils, etc., can help, but only as a last resort following manufacturer instructions!

When it comes to cultivating cannabis, success is all about preparation. Stay on top of your seedlings and watch out for signs of damping off, nutrient deficiencies, or any pests or diseases that might arise. Putting in the effort by taking preventative measures will save you time (and money). You can reap huge rewards with care and patience - so don't be afraid to get your hands dirty! Sooner rather than later, you'll have a thriving crop and be well on your way to becoming a cannabis master.

Transplanting Seedlings

Transplanting cannabis plants is a must if you want them to thrive. To do it successfully, it's important to understand when the seedling is ready for this move - usually around two to four weeks old with a strong root system and at least two or three sets of true leaves. That being said, preparation goes beyond just knowing when your plant requires transplantation: you need to have an appropriate site prepared and use proper techniques so that the transition can go seamlessly.

Signs It's Time to Transplant

Here are some tips on how best to get there:

- **Age**: Check if your seedlings are around 2-4 weeks old. Any younger than that might still be too delicate for transplanting.

- **Root development**: If roots start appearing from the bottom of their pot or winding themselves through the soil, they're likely ready for relocation.

- **True leaves**: Look out for those Cannabis leaf shapes – these indicate that your plant has enough strength (and nutrients) built up to survive moving day.

Once everything's been checked off, all that's left is providing post-transplant care, such as keeping moisture levels stable and monitoring growth closely until you see healthy signs of progress again (i.e., more new leaves).

1. **Preparing the Transplant Site**

Ready to transplant your cannabis seedlings? Here's what you need to know.

- **Pick the right pot**: Depending on the size of your plant, find a 3–5-gallon container for smaller plants and 7-10 gallons for larger ones. This way, there'll be plenty of room for growth!

- **Select soil wisely**: Quality is key here - look out for nutrient-rich soil that'll help ensure proper development in your cannabis seedling. Plus, make sure it drains well so roots don't get waterlogged!

- **Pre-moisten substrate**: Before putting everything together, moisten up the growing medium to provide hydration immediately once transplanted - this will reduce shock and encourage speedy root establishment too!

- **Create a perfect hole**: When planting time comes around, dig a hole with enough space to fit the entire root ball snugly inside without any damage during the transferal process.

Transplanting Techniques

Proper transplanting is key to keeping cannabis seedlings happy and healthy. Here's how to do it right:

- **Water them**: Give your little sprouts a nice drink before you start the move. This helps keep their root ball intact when it's time for lift-off.

- **Prepare for takeoff**: Carefully remove the seedling from its original container - use a tool or your fingers if need be - take care not to damage any delicate roots in the process.

- **Plant with precision**: Place your young plant in its new home, ensuring that the top of its root ball is level with the surrounding soil so it can settle into its surroundings properly.

- **Fill them up**: Gently backfill around them, ensuring no air pockets are left behind. Give everything a light press down so they feel secure and supported!

- **Drench them**: Thoroughly water both old and new homes alike to reduce any shock from being uprooted – that'll help them get settled quickly too!

2. **Post-Transplant Care**

When it comes to giving your cannabis seedlings the best chance of survival, proper care after transplanting is key. Here's how you can ensure your new plant babies get off on the right foot and flourish in their new home.

- **Humidity**: Keeping a humidity level between 60-70% for at least the first week will give newly transplanted plants some serious care and love - use a humidifier or take advantage of an enclosed environment like a humidity dome if needed!

- **Temperature Control**: The temperature should stay consistent, somewhere around 68-77°F (20-25°C). This gives them just enough warmth while avoiding stress due to drastic changes in temp.

- **Light Intensity**: When introducing them into their new digs, ease up on light intensity or increase the distance from grow lights for 24-48 hours until they've adjusted.

- **Water Carefully**: To promote root growth and prevent overwatering, only water when the topsoil has dried out about an inch down from the surface.

Taking all these steps means you're well on your way toward cultivating healthy and lush cannabis plants that'll make any weed enthusiast proud - just remember to be gentle with those fragile young sprouts throughout this crucial time in their development!

Common Mistakes

Transplanting cannabis seedlings is a delicate process that requires attention and finesse. Falls in the wrong direction can spell disaster for your plants, so knowing what missteps you need to avoid is important. Here are some common mistakes when transplanting cannabis seedlings:

- **Do not plant too early or late:** If you try to move your plant too soon without adequate root systems and at least two sets of true leaves, stress will set in and stunt their growth. But if you wait too long, roots may become bound, which will also cause issues with health and growth.

- **Be gentle on those roots:** Carefully remove the seedling from its original container handling the root ball gently - any damage caused here can lead straight into "transplant shock," resulting in reduced growth rates.

- **Prepare the site accordingly:** Make sure container size and growing medium are spot on before planting. Plus, pre-moisten the soil appropriately, as this helps reduce stress levels during transition time.

- **Don't dig deep or shallow:** Burying them too deep means possible stem rot, while not digging enough results in poor development throughout roots. So aim for level par between the surrounding soil and the top part of the root ball.

- **Water wisely:** Overwatering results in oxygen deprivation and potential root rot, while underwatering causes wilting. So keep a good watering schedule, ensuring the top inch dries off before rehydrating again.

- **Ignoring aftercare:** Don't skimp on post-transplant care! It's essential for your seedlings to get back on their feet and stay healthy. Create the right atmosphere - maintain optimal humidity, temperature, and lighting levels. Then keep an eye out for any visible signs of distress or disease.

- **Exposing seedlings to extremes:** Bright light and strong winds can be too much for newly transplanted babies. Take it easy by introducing them slowly to their new environment with gentler lighting conditions and shielding them from gusts in the early days.

- **Not monitoring for pests and diseases:** Stress can make plants more vulnerable to pests or illnesses, so regular checks are key if you want your cannabis crop in tip-top condition all season long! Follow these simple steps, and you'll be well on your way toward a successful transplant journey with lushly growing plants that are fit as a fiddle.

Chapter 5: Vegetative Growth and Plant Training Techniques

Vegetative growth is an essential part of the cannabis plant's life cycle - it's where these greens lay the groundwork for producing top-notch buds. This chapter covers why vegetative growth matters, how to set up your plants for successful flowering, and what strategies growers can use to ensure maximum yield.

Getting off on the right foot is key! During this stage, roots spread out to absorb nutrients and water more efficiently - helping protect against any future environmental stressors.

Plus, as leaf production increases, photosynthetic capacity goes up too, providing ample energy during bud development later down the line. Additionally, structural developments are paramount when aiming for large dense nugs come harvest time! Having a strong foundation from start to finish will lead you to better yields all around! So don't forget those training techniques if you want great results.

5. *Cannabis plant in a vegetative growth stage.
Source: J. Patrick Bedell, Public domain, via
Wikimedia Commons:*
*https://commons.wikimedia.org/wiki/File:Cannabis-vegetative-growth-
00003.jpg*

The Role of Vegetative Growth in Laying the Groundwork for Spectacular Blooms

It's essential for a healthy yield that your plants get off to an awesome start during their vegetative phase. Here are some of the major perks that come with giving them a strong foundation:

- **Grow those roots:** A powerful root system lets plants absorb nutrients and water more effectively, both necessities in getting buds all nice 'n juicy.

- **Beef up that structure:** To make sure your crops can hold up big blooms as they grow, you'll want to ensure sturdy branches and stems are in place from the get-go.

- **Maximize light exposure through canopy formation:** Setting up a good canopy ensures every part of your plant gets its fair share of sunlight to reach peak performance for maximum flowerage.

- **Make sure your plants are ready for anything life throws at them:** If you've already put effort into making sure vegetation is off to an epic beginning, then it should be able to handle any kind of challenge that comes later on down the line like pests or environmental changes - no sweat!

The Duration of the Vegetative Stage

The vegetative growth stage of cannabis plants can vary dramatically - it all depends on the strain, environment, and grower preferences. So let's break down these three elements:

- **Strain**: Indica strains are usually done in 2-4 weeks. Sativas typically need a bit more time to reach their flowering stage (around 4-6 weeks). Auto flowers don't even play by the same rules – they have their own predetermined vegetative period, which is usually shorter than other types (2-4 weeks).

- **Growing Conditions**: The atmosphere surrounding your plant greatly affects how long its veg cycle will be. Light intensity, temperature control, humidity levels, and nutrient distribution all factor into this equation. Provide quality conditions for optimal growth, and you may have a quicker transition from vegetation to flowering!

- **Grower Preferences**: This is where things get interesting – depending on individual goals when growing marijuana, there are multiple paths one might take concerning extending/shortening the duration of vegetation. If size matters, then longer periods could be beneficial as it allows for larger plants that yield higher bud sites at harvest time. However, if the height needs restraining, opt for less greenery before entering flower mode!

Optimizing Light Cycles for Vegetative Growth

When it comes to cannabis growth and development, light is a major player. Photosynthesis - the process of converting light into energy necessary for life's functions (growth, maintenance, and reproduction) - relies on this luminous resource as its primary source. But that isn't all; photoperiodism also plays an essential role in regulating plant development by responding to changes in day length. To optimize vegetative growth and maximize yields from your crop, getting familiar with how different light cycles affect your plants is key.

Cannabis plants are most often classified as short-day flora because they require uninterrupted darkness for flowering initiation; long-day varieties need specific durations of daylight instead, while day-neutral species don't rely on the time of day at all. During the vegetation stage, though, ample lighting should be provided to not trigger premature blooming yet still promote strong growth spurts.

Light cycling for vegetative growth in cannabis plants is a big deal – and there are three main options you should know. First, the classic 18/6: eighteen hours of light followed by six hours of darkness. Then, 20/4 – twenty hours of light with four dark. Lastly, 24/0 continuous lighting with no break between day and night cycles. Each has pros and cons depending on what kind of strain you're growing, your climate conditions, your level of energy usage, etcetera. So it's important to do your research before making any decisions!

If you're looking for the fastest vegetation growth possible, then 24/0 is the light cycle for you. But this intense regimen should only be attempted by experienced growers because of its high-power demand. Not to mention, some strains may not appreciate being deprived of their much-needed rest!

A more balanced option is 18/6 – a popular pick among green thumbs that mimics summer's natural day length and offers plants ample opportunity to grow while conserving energy. The six hours of darkness also allow them to carry out vital metabolic processes.

The 20/4 schedule can also provide healthy yields, but it comes with an increased energy bill at the end of each month! So if your goal is strong vegetative growth without draining your wallet dry, then 18/6 could be just what you need – perfect harmony between productivity and efficiency.

Ensuring optimal growth of your cannabis plants starts with understanding the importance of light and photoperiodism. To help maximize yield potential, it's essential to customize the intensity, spectrum, and distance between the light source and plant canopy during their vegetative stage. More blue-light is necessary for strong stems and leaves, while carefully monitoring this distance can avoid too much heat or burn.

Don't let your plants go up in smoke - remember that managing vegetative growth correctly sets you up for a successful flowering period! Achieving this requires an appropriate balance between lighting conditions so there are no nutrient deficiencies or stress on the crop. So take some time to review how best to adjust these factors according to your grow space, then reap those sweet rewards come harvest season.

Nutrient Requirements and Feeding Schedules

The health, growth, and development of cannabis plants heavily depend on proper nutrition. During the vegetative stage, providing them with a balanced mix of macronutrients and micronutrients is key to achieving vigorous growth that will prepare them for flowering.

Understanding which elements are necessary for success - nitrogen (N), phosphorus (P), potassium (K), calcium (Ca), magnesium (Mg), sulfur(S), as well as iron (Fe), manganese (Mn), zinc (Zn), copper (Cu) boron (B), molybdenum (Mo), and chlorine (Cl) —and how to provide an appropriate nutrient solution is essential to maximize potential yield during cultivation.

Nutrition plays a major role in the entire life cycle of cannabis plants. Each element has its vital part in aiding their growth and development. Macronutrients must be available in larger amounts, while trace amounts of micronutrients will support strong root systems leading up to healthy foliage that can withstand any environment or stressors it may face come harvest time.

During the vegetative stage, cannabis plants have particular nutrient requirements that differ from those of the blooming phase. Nitrogen is especially essential here as it's a key player in photosynthesis and protein formation - acting to synthesize chlorophyll and amino acids alike. Phosphorus aids root growth, energy transfer, and multiple metabolic processes, while potassium facilitates water/nutrient absorption and overall plant health.

Creating a nutrient solution perfectly calibrated for optimal vegetative growth requires careful consideration. It's all about having the right balance of nitrogen, phosphorus, and potassium - typically expressed as an N-P-K ratio like 3-1-2 or 2-1-2. This provides your veggie plants with just enough nutrients to flourish without overloading them; after all, too much (or not enough) of any one element can stunt their growth. So it pays to get the mix just right!

As plants grow during their vegetative stage, it is key to monitor them closely—keeping an eye out for nutrient deficiencies or excesses. Doing so allows growers to make the necessary adjustments to maximize plant performance. To identify potential issues, pay attention to signs like yellowing of the lower leaves (a sign of nitrogen deficiency) and dark purple/blue coloration on leaves (which could indicate a phosphorus deficiency). On the other hand, if you notice leaf tip burn or any other forms of stress, there may be too many nutrients present, thus requiring a reduction in concentration levels. Make sure your crops stay healthy by staying one step ahead!

Pruning Techniques for Healthy Vegetative Growth

Pruning is essential to proper cannabis cultivation - it's the key to growing strong, healthy plants with maximum yield potential. Cultivators can easily control how their plant grows and flourishes by nipping off leaves, branches, and buds strategically. Furthermore, pruning helps promote air circulation within the canopy while reducing the risk of diseases or pests - all of which adds up to a healthier harvest!

When it comes to pruning your cannabis crop, there are several techniques at your disposal: Topping, Defoliation, and Lolli popping – each one has its purpose, as well as when and how often it should be done for ideal results. So if you want monster-sized yields come harvest time, then knowing when (and what) to prune is crucial. Let's break down these three methods so you know just what's needed from now until flower power kicks in:

Topping: Topping is a pruning technique that can make your plants thrive. It involves snipping off the plant's apical meristem, or main growing tip, to encourage more primary branches. This creates a denser and more compact structure with increased bud sites leading to potentially higher yields. Topping helps evenly distribute growth hormones throughout the plant, promoting balanced growth. So don't be afraid to give your green friends a trim. You just might get some sweet rewards in return.

Defoliation: Shedding leaves from the marijuana plant is a careful process. Defoliation targets mature, larger-sized foliage that may block light or airflow to lower growth points. Doing this will provide better light penetration and airflow - encouraging even distribution of nutrients across the whole canopy and reducing potential risks for diseases or pests. To get optimal results, defoliate slowly and cautiously. Overly aggressive removal can cause stress on your bud baby, decreasing their photosynthetic capacity in turn.

Lolli popping: Get rid of the bottom-tier growth and let your plant soar - that's Lolli popping. This pruning strategy eliminates twigs, branches, and leaves receiving minimal to no light, allowing a plant to focus on energy production through its upper canopy, where maximum sun exposure is achieved. The result is more robust blossoms. By cutting away what holds the plants back, you clear their way for better yields.

Timing and frequency are key when trimming during the vegetative phase since pruning too early, late, or often can have dire consequences on development and growth. It's best to start snipping once plants boast a few true leaves and the root system is firmly established - usually somewhere between the 4th-6th week of vegetation. Regular pruning throughout this period allows for enough recovery time in between sessions for your greenery to adjust accordingly.

In addition to monitoring progress for signs of damage or disease, any affected plant material should be promptly discarded. Leaving it could open up doorways for pests/pathogens that could spread infection and harm overall health.

Essentially, pruning plays an integral role in cannabis cultivation as it affects growth patterns directly while also helping optimize yields with techniques like topping, defoliation, and Lolli popping (just imagine giving your buds a nice little haircut). By plotting out ideal timing/frequency and taking necessary precautions against potential threats, growers can ensure healthy flowers come harvest season that will deliver top-notch quality and reliable yields!

Plant Training Methods for Maximizing Yield Potential

Maximizing your cannabis yield and keeping it primo requires harnessing a few cultivation techniques like Topping, Low-Stress Training (LST), and FIMing. These approaches ensure that every part of the marijuana plant gets proper attention so you can easily reach maximum harvest potential. Taking advantage of light distribution, airflow, and bud growth will help level up your growing game in no time!

The bountiful harvest that awaits you can be yours simply by training your plants the right way! Plant training is a must for achieving an even canopy, improving light absorption, and stimulating lateral growth. With increased sunlight penetration, each bud site will get its fill of energy to produce optimal flowers. So take advantage of this trick and reap the rewards - a balanced system with better photosynthesis capabilities plus enhanced branching and yield potential, all leading to maximum success!

Topping: Ready to take your gardening game up a notch? Topping is an effective pruning technique that maximizes growth potential in plants by removing the top bud (known as apical meristem). This repositions the auxin, a crucial hormone responsible for plant development, which encourages two main colas with more buds and higher yields. For the best results, topping should be done during the vegetative stage, when plants have true leaves and strong roots, thereby giving them enough time to recover before another session.

Low-Stress Training (LST): If you want to take the stress out of tending your plants, then low-stress training could be just the technique for you. Rather than topping or pruning, this method involves bending and tying down branches to create an even canopy - without any cutting required! This ensures that all bud sites get adequate light exposure to grow big and strong with lush flowers come harvest time. Plus, LST encourages lateral growth and secondary branching, which boosts overall yields when done correctly. So if it's a less stressful approach you want for managing your crop, LST is worth considering – but don't forget the soft ties! Keep an eye on things as your plant grows throughout the vegetation stage into early flowering. Slight adjustments may need to be made here and there to keep everything healthy and thriving.

FIMing (F*ck I Missed): Take a break from topping and try this less aggressive technique instead. It involves pinching or cutting about ¾ of the way up the apical meristem, leaving just enough of the tip intact so you don't mess up (hence, "F*ck I Missed"). This method will give your plant more branches while still keeping it compact and efficient - like getting two birds with one stone. It should be done during veg growth once several sets of true leaves have developed and roots are strongly in place. However, make sure to let your plant recover between sessions so no stress is involved.

In a nutshell, mastering the art of plant training is essential for getting those top-shelf nugs. From Topping to Low-Stress Training and FIMing - savvy cultivators know how to shape their plants for maximum light absorption and extra bud sites. Of course, precisely timing each step is paramount – no shortcuts are allowed! Make sure your herb has time to recoup after every process if you want that fire yield to come harvest time. So don't sleep on this cultivation ritual. Give it the attention it deserves and reap those rewards in no time.

Combining Techniques and Monitoring Plant Progress

Cultivating cannabis with finesse? That's a tall order. But don't fret; it can be done - and you'll reap the rewards from your hard work too! To start on the right foot, tailoring each plant's pruning and training plan based on individual needs is key. Next up: monitor the growth and health of your plants regularly so you can make adjustments as needed. And finally, getting them prepped for flowering will yield maximum results come harvest time.

Every step in this process counts if you want an impressive weed haul at the end of all that effort - think of it like assembling a puzzle piece by piece until you've got one beautiful picture! Homing in on details such as adjusting techniques based on feedback from plants, making sure everything aligns for the best yields possible, and being aware of what works better than others will help you achieve success in your cultivation goals.

Growers should know that each cannabis plant has its unique growth patterns, genetic characteristics, and individual responses to training and pruning techniques. That's why cultivators need to keep a close eye on their crop, adapting methods based on each strain's behaviors. Some might thrive with aggressive topping or defoliation, while others may require gentler Low-Stress Training (LST) or minimal pruning practices.

Thus, observing is key to recognizing what works best for your plants!

Monitoring progress is an ongoing process that requires diligence. You should be looking for any signs of stress (wilting leaves, yellowing foliage, stunted growth, etc.), disease/damage issues, and positive changes like increased branching or bud site development. By staying alert about how your ganja is doing at all times, you can adjust strategies accordingly to ensure optimal health and yield potential!

Adjusting techniques and schedules to maximize growth, yield, and health is key to successful cannabis cultivation. For example, if a plant seems overwhelmed post-pruning session, it is wise to give them extra chill time or reduce pruning intensity before the next round. However, if a particular training technique doesn't seem to be doing its job - don't fret! Try another approach or tone down your expectation - thereby striking that perfect balance between optimizing results while keeping your plants stress-free.

Preparing your plants for the transition to flowering can be tricky - one misstep and you could jeopardize their entire development! It's best to gradually reduce training and pruning intensity to ensure a successful bloom as they move into this stage. In other words: give them some space about 1-2 weeks before the big switch so they can focus on making those beautiful flowers. This allows them time to recover from any stress caused by earlier activities while still being well-prepared when it comes time for blooming. Don't risk stunting your plant's progress - say goodbye (for now) to heavy pruning and training once things start getting floral!

In conclusion, when it comes to growing ganja, diligent monitoring and a tailored approach are key. Pruning and training each plant should be handled carefully - you don't want any health issues ruining your growth! As flowering starts, tweaking little things here-and-there will help maximize bud quality while keeping plants healthy. That way, you can stack up on those fire nugs for all your stoney needs!

Chapter 6: Flowering and Bud Development

The flowering stage is a critical period in the life cycle of a cannabis plant. During this phase, the plant produces buds rich in cannabinoids and terpenes, making it highly desirable for both medicinal and recreational users. In this chapter, we will delve into the various aspects of the flowering stage, including the transition from the vegetative stage, factors that influence bud development, and techniques to maximize resin production. We will also discuss the importance of plant structure, monitoring and assessing bud development, and the proper harvesting, drying, and curing methods to ensure optimal bud quality.

6. *Cannabis plant in the flowering stage. Source:*
Matthias Ghidossi, CC BY-SA 4.0

The Transition from Vegetative to Flowering Stage

Before we discuss the transition to flowering, it's essential to understand the vegetative stage.

During this phase, cannabis plants focus on growing taller, developing strong branches and leaves, and establishing a sturdy root system. The vegetative stage is characterized by long hours of light (usually 18 hours on and 6 hours off) and a specific nutrient mix, typically high in nitrogen.

As cannabis plants mature, they will begin to show signs that they are ready to transition into the flowering stage. In photoperiod-sensitive strains, this transition is triggered by a change in the light cycle, while auto-flowering strains will start flowering based on their genetic timeline. Some signs that a cannabis plant is entering the flowering stage include:

- The appearance of pre-flowers, which are small, hair-like structures on the plant's nodes

- A rapid increase in plant height, often referred to as "the stretch"

- A change in leaf morphology, with leaves becoming narrower and more elongated

Adjusting Lighting Schedules for Flowering

To initiate flowering in photoperiod-sensitive cannabis plants, the light schedule must be adjusted to provide them with longer periods of darkness. Typically, this involves changing the light cycle from 18 hours of light and 6 hours of darkness (18/6) to 12 hours of light and 12 hours of darkness (12/12). This change mimics the natural shift in daylight hours that occurs as the seasons change, signaling to the plant that it's time to start producing flowers. Auto-flowering strains, on the other hand, do not require a change in the light cycle to begin flowering.

Modifying Nutrient Requirements

As cannabis plants enter the flowering stage, their nutrient requirements change. While the vegetative stage demands high nitrogen levels to support rapid growth, the flowering stage requires a different nutrient mix to develop healthy buds. Plants need higher phosphorus and potassium levels during flowering, while nitrogen levels should be reduced. Many commercial nutrient lines offer specific formulations designed for the flowering stage, making it easy to adjust the nutrient mix to meet the needs of your plants. Ensuring proper nutrient ratios will help support optimal bud development and overall plant health during the flowering stage.

Factors Influencing Bud Development

These are some factors that influence bud development:

Light Intensity and Spectrum

Light plays a crucial role in the development of cannabis buds. During the flowering stage, plants require strong, intense light to produce bud formation and growth energy. Light intensity is measured in photosynthetically active radiation (PAR), with values between 500 and 1000 $\mu mol/m^2/s$ typically considered optimal for flowering cannabis plants. Lower PAR values can result in reduced bud size and potency, while excessively high PAR values can lead to light stress and damage the plants.

The light spectrum is also an important factor during flowering. Cannabis plants benefit from a spectrum rich in red and far-red wavelengths, which promote flower development and increase yield. Many growers use high-pressure sodium (HPS) lights, LED lights, or a combination of both to provide the ideal spectrum for flowering cannabis plants.

Temperature and Humidity Control

Maintaining appropriate temperature and humidity levels is essential for healthy bud development. During the flowering stage, cannabis plants prefer slightly cooler temperatures than in the vegetative stage, with daytime temperatures between 68-77°F (20-25°C) and nighttime temperatures around 59-68°F (15-20°C). These cooler temperatures help to preserve terpenes and cannabinoids while minimizing the risk of mold and mildew.

Humidity levels should also be lowered during flowering, ideally to around 40-50% relative humidity (RH). Lower humidity levels help to reduce the risk of mold and mildew, especially in the dense buds that cannabis plants produce. Proper airflow and ventilation are also important in maintaining an optimal growing environment with consistent temperature and humidity levels.

Nutrient Ratios and Feeding Schedule

As mentioned earlier, cannabis plants require different nutrient ratios during their flowering stage. Higher phosphorus and potassium levels are needed to support bud development, while nitrogen should be reduced. A balanced nutrient mix is essential for optimal bud growth, resin production, and overall plant health.

In addition to adjusting nutrient ratios, modifying the feeding schedule during the flowering stage is crucial. As plants progress through the flowering stage, their nutrient requirements will change. Early in the flowering stage, they may still benefit from some nitrogen, while later in the stage, they will require higher amounts of phosphorus and potassium. It's essential to monitor your plants and adjust your nutrient schedule accordingly to meet their changing needs.

Some growers also employ a technique called "flushing" in the final weeks before harvest. Flushing involves providing the plants with plain water, with no added nutrients, to help remove any residual nutrients from the plant tissue. This process can improve the taste and smoothness of the final product, as excess nutrients can contribute to a harsh, unpleasant flavor.

Maximizing Resin Production

The resin produced by cannabis plants contains the valuable cannabinoids and terpenes that are sought after for their medicinal and recreational properties. In this section, you will learn the importance of resin production and explore various techniques to maximize resin production, including defoliation, pruning, and the use of bloom boosters. These methods can help enhance the potency, aroma, and overall quality of your cannabis buds.

Importance

Resin is a sticky substance secreted by the trichomes, tiny hair-like structures that cover the cannabis plant's flowers and leaves. This resin contains the cannabinoids, such as THC and CBD, and terpenes, which give cannabis its unique aroma and flavor profiles. Maximizing resin production is crucial for growers, as it directly impacts the potency, quality, and overall value of the cannabis buds.

Techniques for Boosting Resin Production

There are several techniques that growers can employ to optimize resin production in cannabis plants. These methods can help improve the overall quality and potency of the final product.

1. Defoliation

Defoliation is the process of removing some of the fan leaves from a cannabis plant. Defoliation aims to increase light penetration and airflow to the lower buds, thereby promoting more even and robust bud development. This technique can also help increase resin production by directing more of the plant's energy toward the buds rather than the leaves. Defoliation should be done carefully and selectively, as removing too many leaves can stress the plant and reduce overall yield.

2. Pruning

Pruning involves the selective removal of specific branches or buds from the cannabis plant. This technique can be used to shape the plant, encourage a more even canopy, and improve light penetration to the lower buds. Pruning can also help to maximize resin production by focusing the plant's energy on the remaining buds, leading to larger and more resinous flowers. Pruning should be done gradually over several weeks rather than all at once to avoid stressing the plant.

3. Bloom boosters

Bloom boosters are nutrient supplements specifically designed to enhance flower production and resin output in cannabis plants. These products typically contain high levels of phosphorus, potassium, and other beneficial ingredients like amino acids, vitamins, and trace minerals. By providing targeted nutrition during the flowering stage, bloom boosters can support optimal bud development and increased resin production. It is essential to follow the manufacturer's instructions when using bloom boosters and monitor your plants' overall health, as overuse can lead to nutrient imbalances and other issues.

Implementing these techniques and carefully monitoring your plants can optimize resin production, leading to higher quality, more potent, and aromatic cannabis buds.

Monitoring and Assessing Bud Development

Keeping a close eye on your cannabis plants during the flowering stage is crucial for ensuring healthy bud development and identifying any potential issues. Now you will know about the signs of healthy bud development, common problems that can arise, and the role of trichomes in determining the optimal harvest time.

Healthy cannabis buds will exhibit several key characteristics, including:

- **Steady growth**: Buds should continue to grow in size and density throughout the flowering stage.

- **Dense structure**: Well-developed buds will be dense and tightly packed, with minimal gaps between the individual flowers.

- **Rich aroma**: As the buds mature and the terpene content increases, they should develop a strong, distinct aroma.

- **Vibrant coloration**: Depending on the strain, healthy buds may exhibit various colors, such as deep greens, purples, or even blues, with bright orange or brown pistils.

- **Trichome development**: The trichomes, which contain cannabinoids and terpenes, should become more numerous and pronounced as the buds mature.

Common Issues

During the flowering stage, several issues can affect bud development, including:

- **Nutrient deficiencies or imbalances**: These can manifest in various ways, such as yellowing leaves, slow growth, or poor bud development. To address nutrient issues, monitor your plants closely and adjust your feeding schedule and nutrient mix as needed.

- **Pests and diseases**: Common cannabis pests like spider mites, aphids, and whiteflies, as well as diseases like powdery mildew and bud rot, can significantly impact bud health. Implement preventative measures, such as proper hygiene and airflow, and promptly treat any infestations or infections to minimize damage.

- **Environmental factors**: Suboptimal temperature, humidity, and light conditions can reduce bud quality and yield. Monitor your grow environment closely and adjust as needed to maintain optimal conditions.

Chapter 7: Harvesting and Drying Cannabis

After months of nurturing and care, your cannabis plants have finally reached maturity, and it's time to harvest the fruits of your labor. This chapter will walk you through the crucial stages of harvesting, drying, and curing your cannabis buds to ensure optimal quality, potency, and flavor. You will start by knowing the signs of plant maturity and readiness for harvest, then delve into different harvesting techniques, trimming methods, and step-by-step instructions for proper drying and curing.

7. *Cannabis drying room. Source: Beeblebrox, CC BY-SA 4.0* <https://creativecommons.org/licenses/by-sa/4.0>, via

Recognizing Plant Maturity and Harvest Readiness

Before you can harvest your cannabis plants, it's essential to determine whether they have reached full maturity and are ready for harvest. Harvesting too early or too late can significantly impact the final product's potency, flavor, and overall quality.

Cannabis plants show several indicators of maturity, which can help guide your decision on when to harvest. Some common signs of plant maturity include:

- **Pistil color**: The pistils, or hair-like structures on the cannabis flowers, will change color as the plant matures. They typically start as white and transition to an orange or brown hue when the plant is nearing maturity.

- **Swelling of calyxes**: The calyxes, or individual flower structures, will swell and become more pronounced as the plant matures.

- **Slowing of vertical growth**: Cannabis plants will generally stop growing taller and focus their energy on bud development during the flowering stage. When vertical growth has ceased, this is often an indicator that the plant is nearing maturity.

- **Yellowing of fan leaves**: As the plant diverts nutrients and energy towards bud development, the fan leaves may begin to yellow and fall off, signaling that the plant is reaching the end of its life cycle.

Analyzing Trichomes

While the above signs can provide a general sense of plant maturity, examining the trichomes is the most accurate method for determining the optimal harvest window. Trichomes are tiny, crystal-like structures that cover the cannabis buds and contain the cannabinoids and terpenes responsible for the plant's effects and flavor.

As the cannabis plant matures, the trichomes will change in appearance, transitioning from clear to cloudy and eventually to amber. This change in color corresponds to the peak potency of the cannabinoids and terpenes within the trichomes. You will need a jeweler's loupe or a microscope to examine the trichomes.

Most growers aim to harvest when the majority of the trichomes are cloudy, with some turning amber. This typically results in buds with the highest potency and the most well-rounded terpene profile. However, personal preferences and desired effects may influence the precise timing of the harvest. For example, harvesting when more trichomes have turned amber may result in a more sedative, body-focused effect, while harvesting earlier with clearer trichomes may yield a more cerebral, energetic high.

By recognizing the signs of plant maturity and analyzing the trichomes, you can determine the optimal harvest window for your cannabis plants, ensuring the best possible potency, flavor, and overall quality of your buds.

Harvest Preparation

Before diving into the actual process of harvesting your cannabis plants, it's essential to prepare your tools, workspace, and organization system properly. Proper preparation makes the harvesting process more efficient and helps prevent contamination and damage to your buds.

Before you begin harvesting, gather the following tools and equipment:

- **Pruning shears or scissors**: Sharp, clean pruning shears or scissors are essential for cutting branches or individual buds from the plant. Choose a pair that feels comfortable in your hand and provides precise cuts.

- **Gloves**: Wear disposable gloves to protect your hands from the sticky resin and to prevent any contaminants from coming into contact with your cannabis.

- **Trimming scissors**: Smaller, precise trimming scissors are ideal for removing leaves and manicuring your buds during the trimming process.

- **Clean, flat surface**: A large, clean, flat surface like a table or countertop is helpful for laying out your harvested branches and for trimming.

- **Storage containers or bags**: Large paper bags, plastic bins, or trays can temporarily store your trimmed buds before moving on to the drying stage.

- **Labels and markers**: Labeling your branches or buds with strain names or other relevant information is crucial for keeping track of your harvest, especially if you're growing multiple strains or plants.

Sanitizing Tools and Workspace

Sanitizing your tools and workspace is essential in the harvest preparation process. Clean, sanitized tools help to prevent the transfer of any contaminants, mold, or pathogens to your cannabis buds. To sanitize your tools, use rubbing alcohol or a tool sterilization solution, and make sure to clean your working surface thoroughly with soap and water or a disinfectant. Maintain cleanliness throughout the harvesting process to ensure the health and safety of your buds.

Organizing and Labeling Different Strains or Plants

If you're growing multiple strains or plants, it's important to establish a clear system for organizing and labeling your harvest. This will facilitate easier tracking and identification of your buds during the drying and curing stages.

You can label each branch or bud with a small piece of masking tape and a marker, indicating the strain name and any other necessary information, such as the harvest date. Alternatively, you can use separate containers or bags for each strain or plant, clearly labeling each container with the relevant information.

Proper preparation is key to a successful harvest. By gathering the necessary tools and equipment, sanitizing your workspace, and organizing your cannabis plants, you can ensure a smooth and efficient harvesting process while minimizing the risk of contamination or damage to your buds.

Harvesting Techniques

Determining the best harvesting technique for your cannabis plants is crucial for maximizing yield and quality. This section will discuss two common harvesting techniques – whole plant harvesting and selective or branch-by-branch harvesting – and delve into the pros, cons, and best practices for each method.

Whole Plant Harvesting

Whole plant harvesting involves cutting down the entire cannabis plant at the base of its main stem, then hanging the plant upside down to dry. This technique is relatively straightforward and can be more time-efficient, especially for smaller grows or when dealing with a limited number of plants.

Pros:

- **Simplicity**: Whole plant harvesting is a quick and easy method that requires less initial handling of the plant.

- **Slower drying**: The intact plant structure may slow the drying process, which can help preserve terpenes and potentially improve the final product's flavor profile.

Cons:

- **Inconsistent maturity**: Different parts of the plant may mature at different rates, so harvesting the entire plant at once might result in some buds being over- or under-ripe.

- **Space requirements**: Whole plant harvesting can require more space for drying, as the entire plant must be hung upside down.

Best practices:

- When cutting down the entire plant, make a clean, sharp cut at the base of the main stem using pruning shears or a sharp knife.

- Remove any large fan leaves before hanging the plant to dry, as they can hold moisture and slow down the drying process or potentially contribute to mold growth.

Selective or Branch-by-Branch Harvesting

Selective harvesting involves cutting individual branches or even specific buds from the cannabis plant as they reach maturity. This technique allows for a more precise harvest, as you can target the most mature buds and leave the rest of the plant to continue ripening.

Pros:

- **Harvest precision**: Selective harvesting enables you to harvest only the most mature buds, ensuring optimal ripeness and quality for each harvested section.

- **Staggered harvest**: This technique allows for a staggered harvest, which can help manage workload and drying space more efficiently, especially for larger grows.

Cons:

- **Time-consuming**: Selective harvesting can be more labor-intensive and time-consuming, as each branch or bud must be assessed for maturity and cut individually.

- **Potential stress to the plant**: Repeatedly cutting branches or buds from the plant may cause stress, potentially impacting the plant's overall health and yield.

Best Practices:

- Examine each branch or bud carefully to determine its maturity level, paying close attention to the trichomes and other signs of ripeness discussed above.

- Use sharp, sanitized pruning shears or scissors to make clean cuts when removing branches or buds, not damaging the remaining plant structure.

- Label harvested branches or buds as needed, especially if you are growing multiple strains or plants.

Both whole plant and selective harvesting have advantages and disadvantages, and the best technique for your grow will depend on factors such as your plant size, grow space, and personal preferences. By understanding the pros and cons of each method and following best practices, you can optimize your harvest and ensure the highest possible quality for your cannabis buds.

Trimming and Manicuring Cannabis Buds

Trimming and manicuring your cannabis buds is a crucial step in harvesting that can greatly impact the final product's appearance, potency, and flavor. In this section, you will know about the importance of trimming, the difference between wet and dry trimming, and provide a step-by-step guide to manicuring your cannabis buds to perfection.

Importance of Trimming

Trimming and manicuring your cannabis buds serve several purposes:

- **Aesthetics**: Well-trimmed buds have a more visually appealing and professional appearance, which can be important for personal satisfaction or marketability if you're growing for sale.

- **Potency**: Sugar leaves, the small leaves that grow within and around the buds, contain lower concentrations of cannabinoids than the buds themselves. Removing these leaves can result in a more potent final product.

- **Flavor and smoothness**: Sugar leaves also contain higher concentrations of chlorophyll than buds, which can impact the flavor and smoothness of the smoke.

Proper trimming can lead to a cleaner, more enjoyable smoking experience.

- **Mold prevention**: Trimming helps to remove excess foliage, which can harbor moisture and potentially lead to mold growth during the drying and curing stages.

Wet Trimming vs. Dry Trimming

Cannabis buds can be trimmed immediately after harvesting (wet trimming) or after drying (dry trimming). Each method has its advantages and drawbacks:

1. Wet Trimming:

Pros: Easier to handle (leaves are more pliable), less messy, and can speed up drying.

Cons: More labor-intensive and time-sensitive, as it must be done immediately after harvesting, and can potentially result in a less aromatic final product due to the faster drying time.

2. Dry Trimming:

Pros: Less labor-intensive at the time of harvest, a slower drying process can improve terpene preservation and final product aroma, and easier to trim as leaves curl up when dry.

Cons: Can be more difficult to trim dry, brittle leaves, and increased risk of mold during the drying process due to the presence of excess foliage.

Your choice between wet and dry trimming will depend on factors such as personal preference, available time, and drying space.

Instructions

- **Prepare your workspace**: Set up a clean, flat surface for trimming, and gather your tools, including trimming scissors, gloves, a container or tray for your trimmed buds, and a waste receptacle for discarded leaves.

- **Remove large fan leaves**: If you haven't already done so during harvesting, remove any large fan leaves from the branches or buds, as these do not contain significant amounts of cannabinoids and can impede the drying process.

- **Trim sugar leaves**: Using your trimming scissors, carefully remove the sugar leaves growing within and around the cannabis buds. Trim as close to the bud as possible without cutting into the bud itself. Some growers prefer to leave a small amount of sugar leaves on the buds for added protection during the drying process, while others prefer a tighter trim for a cleaner appearance.

- **Manicure the buds**: Once the sugar leaves are removed, examine each bud for any remaining small leaves or imperfections, and trim as needed to achieve a clean, uniform appearance. Take care not to damage the buds or trichomes during this process.

- **Store trimmed buds**: Place your trimmed buds in a container or on a tray, taking care to keep them separated to allow proper airflow during the drying process. Label your buds, if necessary, especially if you're working with multiple strains or plants.

Proper trimming and manicuring of your cannabis buds is essential for achieving a high-quality final product. By understanding the importance of trimming, choosing the right method for your needs, and following a careful, methodical approach, you can ensure that your cannabis buds look, taste, and smoke their very best.

Drying and Curing Cannabis Buds

Drying and curing your cannabis buds are essential steps in the post-harvest process that can significantly impact the final product's quality, potency, and shelf life. This section will discuss the importance of proper drying and curing, the optimal conditions for each stage, and provide a detailed guide to achieving perfectly dried and cured cannabis buds.

Drying and curing cannabis buds serve several important purposes:

- **Preservation**: Proper drying and curing help to preserve your cannabis buds, extending their shelf life and preventing the growth of mold and bacteria.

- **Potency**: During the curing process, non-psychoactive cannabinoids like THCA are converted to THC, the primary psychoactive compound in cannabis, increasing the buds' potency.

- **Flavor and aroma**: Drying and curing help to break down chlorophyll and other unwanted chemical compounds, resulting in a smoother, more flavorful smoke and a more pronounced aroma.

- **Smoothness**: Properly dried and cured buds produce a smoother, less harsh smoke, making for a more enjoyable smoking experience.

To achieve the best possible results, it's essential to maintain optimal conditions during the drying and curing process:

- **Drying conditions**: A dark, well-ventilated room with a temperature of 60-70°F (15-21°C) and a relative humidity of 45-55% is ideal for drying cannabis buds. These conditions help prevent mold growth while allowing for a slow, even drying process.

- **Curing conditions**: During the curing process, a slightly higher humidity level of 55-62% is ideal, as it allows for the proper breakdown of chlorophyll and other compounds without drying the buds out too quickly.

Step-by-Step Guide

- **Hang or place buds for drying:** After harvesting and trimming your cannabis buds, hang them upside down on a drying rack, clothesline, or other suitable support, ensuring ample space between the buds for proper airflow. Alternatively, you can place the buds on a drying rack or screen, turning them periodically to ensure even drying.

- **Maintain optimal drying conditions**: Monitor the temperature and humidity in your drying space using a thermometer and hygrometer, and adjust as needed to maintain optimal conditions. Ensure the drying space is dark, as light can degrade cannabinoids and terpenes, impacting the final product's potency and flavor.

- **Check for dryness**: The drying process typically takes 7-14 days, depending on factors such as bud size, ambient conditions, and personal preferences. To check for dryness, gently bend the stems of your cannabis buds; if they snap cleanly, they are ready for curing. If the stems still bend without snapping, continue drying until the desired level of dryness is achieved.

- **Trim and place buds in curing containers**: Once your cannabis buds are sufficiently dry, trim any remaining sugar leaves if you haven't done so already. Then, place the buds in airtight containers, such as glass mason jars or specialized curing containers, filling the containers about 75% full to allow for air exchange.

- **Monitor humidity and burp the containers**: Using a small hygrometer placed inside the curing container, monitor the humidity level and adjust as needed to maintain the ideal range of 55-62%. Burp the containers by opening them for a few minutes each day during the first week of curing, and then gradually decrease the frequency to once every few days or as needed. Burping allows for the release of excess moisture and prevents mold and bacteria growth.

- **Cure for at least 2-4 weeks**: The curing process typically takes a minimum of 2-4 weeks but can be extended for several months or more, depending on personal preferences and desired results. A longer cure can result in smoother, more flavorful smoke and improved shelf life. It's essential to monitor the humidity levels and burp the containers throughout the curing process to ensure optimal results.

By understanding the importance of proper drying and curing, maintaining optimal conditions, and following a careful, methodical approach, you can ensure that your cannabis buds are preserved, potent, and enjoyable for consumption. Properly dried and cured cannabis can last for up to two years or more when stored in a cool, dark, and dry environment, allowing you to savor the fruits of your labor long after the harvest.

Storing Cannabis Buds for Longevity and Quality Preservation

Proper storage of your cannabis buds is essential for maintaining their potency, flavor, aroma, and overall quality over time. This section will discuss the factors that can affect cannabis bud quality during storage, the ideal storage conditions, and provide a step-by-step guide to storing your cannabis buds for optimal longevity and preservation.

Several factors can impact the quality of your stored cannabis buds:

- **Light**: Exposure to light, particularly ultraviolet (UV) light, can degrade cannabinoids and terpenes, leading to a loss of potency and flavor.

- **Temperature**: High temperatures can cause cannabinoids and terpenes to break down, while low temperatures can slow the degradation process.

- **Humidity**: Excess humidity can promote mold growth, while low humidity can cause buds to become overly dry and brittle.

- **Air**: Exposure to oxygen can cause oxidation, leading to a loss of potency and degradation of terpenes and other compounds.

Ideal Storage Conditions for Cannabis Buds

To ensure the best possible preservation of your cannabis buds, it's essential to maintain optimal storage conditions:

- **Light**: Store your cannabis buds in a dark environment, away from direct sunlight or other sources of UV light.

- **Temperature**: Maintain a stable temperature of 60-70°F (15-21°C) to preserve cannabinoids and terpenes.

- **Humidity**: Keep the relative humidity in your storage space at 55-62% to prevent mold growth and maintain bud quality.

- **Air**: Store your cannabis buds in airtight containers to limit their exposure to oxygen and slow the oxidation process.

Step-by-Step Guide

- **Choose appropriate storage containers**: Select airtight containers, such as glass mason jars or specialized cannabis storage containers, to protect your buds from light, air, and moisture. Avoid using plastic bags or containers, as they can allow air to pass through and may impart undesirable flavors or odors to your cannabis.

- **Fill containers with cured buds**: Once your cannabis buds have been properly dried and cured, place them in your chosen storage containers, filling the containers about 75% full to allow for some air exchange.

- **Label containers**: Label your containers with pertinent information, such as strain, harvest date, and any other relevant details. This is especially important if you're storing multiple strains or batches.

- **Store containers in a dark, cool, and dry location**: Place your cannabis storage containers in a dark, temperature-controlled, and humidity-controlled environment, such as a closet, cabinet, or dedicated storage space. Avoid storing your cannabis in areas with fluctuating temperatures or humidity levels, such as near heating vents or in damp basements.

- **Monitor storage conditions**: Regularly check the temperature and humidity in your storage space using a thermometer and hygrometer, and adjust as needed to maintain optimal conditions. Also, inspect the cannabis buds for any signs of mold, discoloration, or other issues, and address any problems promptly.

- **Rotate and refresh stored cannabis**: Periodically open your cannabis storage containers to allow air exchange and ensure the buds remain fresh and properly preserved. If you're storing cannabis for extended periods, consider rotating your supply, consuming older buds first to ensure that they don't degrade over time.

Following these guidelines and maintaining optimal storage conditions ensures that your cannabis buds remain potent, flavorful, and enjoyable for up to two years or more. Properly stored cannabis offers a consistently high-quality smoking experience and allows you to make the most of your harvest and enjoy the fruits of your labor long after the growing season has ended.

Troubleshooting Common Cannabis Growing Issues

Growing cannabis can be a rewarding and enjoyable experience, but it's not without its challenges. This section will discuss common cannabis growing issues and their possible causes and provide solutions to help you address these problems and keep your plants healthy and thriving.

1. Yellowing leaves

Yellowing leaves can indicate several issues, including nutrient deficiencies, overwatering, or pH imbalances.

Possible causes: Nitrogen deficiency, overwatering, or improper pH levels.

Solutions: Adjust your feeding schedule to provide the appropriate nutrients, ensure proper watering practices, and monitor and maintain the pH levels of your growing medium and nutrient solution.

2. Curling or clawing leaves

Curling or clawing leaves can indicate stress, nutrient toxicity, or heat stress.

Possible causes: Over-fertilization, high temperatures, or insufficient airflow.

Solutions: Reduce the amount of nutrients you're feeding your plants, provide adequate ventilation, and maintain optimal temperature and humidity levels in your grow space.

3. Wilting or drooping leaves

Wilting or drooping leaves can be a sign of overwatering, underwatering, or root issues.

Possible causes: Overwatering, underwatering, or root problems such as root rot or root-bound plants.

Solutions: Adjust your watering practices to ensure proper moisture levels, inspect the roots for issues, and transplant root-bound plants to larger containers if necessary.

4. Brown spots or rust-colored spots on leaves

Brown spots or rust-colored spots on leaves can indicate nutrient deficiencies or pests.

Possible causes: Calcium or magnesium deficiency or pests such as spider mites or fungus gnats.

Solutions: Adjust your feeding schedule to provide the necessary nutrients, and inspect your plants for pests, treating them as needed with appropriate pest control methods.

5. Slow or stunted growth

Slow or stunted growth can be caused by a variety of factors, including insufficient light, nutrient imbalances, or poor growing conditions.

Possible causes: Inadequate light, nutrient deficiencies or imbalances, or suboptimal temperature and humidity levels.

Solutions: Ensure your plants receive sufficient light, provide the appropriate nutrients, and maintain optimal temperature and humidity levels in your grow space.

6. Bud rot or mold

Bud rot or mold can be caused by excess moisture, high humidity, or poor airflow.

Possible causes: Excess moisture, high humidity levels, or inadequate airflow.

Solutions: Improve airflow in your grow space, maintain optimal humidity levels, and avoid overwatering your plants.

7. Pests

Pests such as spider mites, aphids, and thrips can cause significant damage to your cannabis plants.

Possible causes: Poor sanitation, the introduction of infested plants or materials, or insufficient pest control measures.

Solutions: Maintain a clean grow space, inspect new plants and materials for pests, and implement appropriate pest control methods.

By proactively monitoring your cannabis plants' health and addressing any issues promptly, you can minimize the impact of these common problems and ensure a successful, bountiful harvest. Remember that growing cannabis is a learning process, and as you gain experience and knowledge, you'll become better equipped to troubleshoot and resolve issues that may arise in your garden.

Harvesting, Drying, and Curing Cannabis for Maximum Potency and Flavor

To achieve the best results from your cannabis plants, it's essential to harvest them at the right time and to dry and cure the buds properly. This process is crucial for enhancing the potency, flavor, and aroma of your cannabis.

Determining the optimal time to harvest your cannabis plants can be challenging, as it depends on the specific strain, growing conditions, and individual preferences. However, there are some general guidelines you can follow:

- **Pistil**: One way to determine when to harvest is by observing the color of the pistils (hair-like structures) on the cannabis buds. When around 50-70% of the pistils have turned from white to brown or red, it's generally a sign that your plants are ready for harvest.

- **Trichome**: A more accurate method for determining the optimal harvest time is by examining the color of the trichomes (small, resin-producing glands) on the cannabis buds. Use a magnifying glass or microscope to observe the trichomes and look for the following color changes:

  - **Clear trichomes**: Your plants are not yet ready for harvest.

  - **Milky or cloudy trichomes**: Your plants are approaching their peak potency and are ready for harvest.

  - **Amber trichomes**: Your plants have reached peak potency, and harvesting at this stage will result in a more sedative, relaxing effect.

Drying Your Cannabis Buds

Properly drying your cannabis buds is essential for preserving their potency, flavor, and aroma. Follow these steps to ensure a successful drying process:

- **Trim your buds**: After harvesting your cannabis plants, trim off any large fan leaves and remove any excess plant material.

- **Hang your buds to dry**: Hang the trimmed buds upside down in a dark, well-ventilated room with a temperature of 60-70°F (15-21°C) and a relative humidity of 45-55%. This environment will promote a slow, even drying process, which is crucial for preserving the buds' quality.

- **Monitor the drying process**: Check your cannabis buds regularly to ensure they're drying evenly and to prevent any mold or mildew from forming. The drying process typically takes 7-14 days, depending on the environmental conditions and the size of the buds.

- **Check for dryness**: You'll know your cannabis buds are dry when the smaller stems snap cleanly when bent rather than bending or folding. The larger stems should still have some flexibility.

Curing Your Cannabis Buds

Curing your cannabis buds is the final step in harvesting and is essential for enhancing their potency, flavor, and aroma. Follow these steps to cure your cannabis buds properly:

- **Trim and manicure your buds**: Once your buds are dry, trim off any remaining leaves and manicure them to their desired shape.

- **Place your buds in airtight containers**: Place your trimmed, dry buds in airtight containers, such as glass mason jars or specialized cannabis storage containers. Fill the containers about 75% full, allowing for some air exchange.

- **Store your containers in a cool, dark place**: Place your containers in a cool, dark location, such as a closet or cabinet, to protect them from light and temperature fluctuations.

- **Burp your containers**: During the first 1-2 weeks of curing, open your containers for 15-30 minutes daily to allow for air exchange and release any built-up moisture. This process is known as "burping" your containers.

- **Monitor the curing process**: After the initial 1-2 weeks, continue to burp your containers once a week and monitor the smell and texture of your cannabis buds. Properly cured cannabis buds should have a pleasant aroma and should not feel overly moist or dry.

- **Cure for at least 2-4 weeks**: The optimal curing time will vary depending on the strain and your personal preferences, but most cannabis buds will benefit from a minimum of 2-4 weeks of curing. Some strains may benefit from even longer curing times, up to several months.

By following these guidelines and properly harvesting, drying, and curing your cannabis buds, you can ensure that they reach their maximum potency and deliver the best possible flavor, aroma, and overall experience. Taking the time and effort to complete these steps carefully will result in a high-quality product that you can be proud of and enjoy.

Storing Cannabis for Long-Term Freshness and Potency

Follow these steps:

- **Prepare your cannabis for storage**: Make sure your cannabis is properly dried and cured before storing it. This will help to prevent mold and mildew growth and ensure optimal potency and flavor.

- **Choose an appropriate storage container**: Use airtight containers made from materials that do not react with or alter the cannabis. Glass jars with airtight seals, such as mason jars, are an excellent choice. Avoid using plastic bags or containers, as they can release chemicals and odors that may affect the quality of your cannabis.

- **Control humidity levels**: To maintain the ideal humidity level inside your storage container, consider using humidity control packs, such as Boveda or Integra Boost packs. These packs are designed to maintain a specific RH level and can be placed directly in your storage container with your cannabis.

- **Label your containers**: If you're storing multiple strains or harvest dates, label your containers with the strain name, harvest date, and any other relevant information. This will help you keep track of your cannabis and ensure you're using the freshest product first.

- **Store your cannabis in a cool, dark place**: Keep your cannabis storage containers in a cool, dark location, such as a closet, cabinet, or basement. Avoid storing your cannabis near heat sources, such as radiators or appliances, as this can cause temperature fluctuations and degrade your cannabis.

- **Keep your cannabis separate from other items**: Store your cannabis away from strong-smelling items or substances, as cannabis can absorb odors and flavors from its surroundings. Additionally, avoid storing your cannabis with items that could introduce contaminants or pests.

- **Check your cannabis periodically**: Inspect your stored cannabis periodically to ensure it remains in good condition. Look for signs of mold, mildew, or pests, and address any issues immediately. If you're using humidity control packs, replace them as needed to maintain proper humidity levels.

- **Rotate your stock**: If you have multiple containers or harvests, use a first-in, first-out (FIFO) system to ensure you're using the oldest cannabis first and maintaining the freshness of your stock.

By following these steps and maintaining the ideal storage conditions, you can preserve the potency, flavor, and aroma of your cannabis for an extended period. Properly stored cannabis can remain fresh and potent for up to two years or more, depending on the quality of the initial product and adherence to optimal storage practices.

Chapter 8: Cannabis Extraction Methods and Products

Cannabis extraction is a process that separates and isolates the valuable compounds found in cannabis plants, such as cannabinoids and terpenes. Extraction aims to create a concentrated and pure product for various applications, including medical, recreational, and therapeutic uses. The extracted compounds can be used to make a wide range of cannabis products, such as concentrates, oils, tinctures, edibles, and topicals. This chapter will provide an overview of various extraction methods and discuss the creation of different cannabis products.

8. *Trainwreck bubble hash cannabis sativa gotten using the ice-extraction method. Source: Mjpresson, CC BY-SA 3.0 <https://creativecommons.org/licenses/by-sa/3.0>, via Wikimedia Commons: https://commons.wikimedia.org/wiki/File:American_medical_hashish(7).jpg*

The Importance of Extracting Cannabinoids and Terpenes

Cannabinoids are a group of compounds found in cannabis plants that interact with the human endocannabinoid system to produce various effects. The most well-known cannabinoids are tetrahydrocannabinol (THC), which is responsible for the psychoactive effects of cannabis, and cannabidiol (CBD), which has numerous therapeutic applications without the psychoactive effects. Terpenes are another group of compounds found in cannabis plants that contribute to the plant's aroma and flavor and offer potential therapeutic benefits.

Extraction allows for isolating and concentrating these valuable compounds, making it possible to create cannabis products with specific desired effects, potencies, and flavors. By extracting cannabinoids and terpenes, manufacturers can optimize the cannabis experience for consumers and patients.

Solvent-Based Extraction

Solvent-based extraction is a popular method for extracting cannabinoids and terpenes from cannabis plant material. This method involves using solvents, such as butane, propane, or ethanol, to dissolve the desired compounds from the plant material, creating a concentrated solution. The solvent is then separated from the cannabis extract, leaving a pure and potent product behind.

There are several solvent-based extraction techniques, including:

- **Butane Hash Oil (BHO) extraction**: This method uses butane as the primary solvent to extract cannabinoids and terpenes from the cannabis plant material. The butane and cannabis mixture is then purged using heat and vacuum to remove the residual solvent, resulting in a highly concentrated extract known as BHO.

- **Propane Hash Oil (PHO) extraction**: Similar to BHO extraction, PHO extraction uses propane as the solvent instead of butane. The process is nearly identical to BHO extraction, but the resulting product has a different consistency and flavor profile due to the use of propane.

- **Ethanol extraction**: This method uses ethanol as the solvent to dissolve cannabinoids and terpenes from the cannabis plant material. After the extraction process, the ethanol is evaporated or filtered out, leaving behind a concentrated cannabis extract.

1. **Common solvents used**

The most common solvents used in cannabis extraction are:

- **Butane**: A highly efficient solvent, butane is widely used in the production of cannabis concentrates due to its ability to dissolve a large number of cannabinoids and terpenes while leaving behind minimal plant material. Butane is also relatively easy to purge from the final product.

- **Propane**: Like butane, propane is an efficient solvent that can extract a significant number of cannabinoids and terpenes. Propane's lower boiling point can result in a different consistency and flavor profile in the final product compared to butane.

- **Ethanol**: A polar solvent, ethanol can extract both water-soluble and fat-soluble compounds, making it a versatile choice for cannabis extraction. However, ethanol can also extract chlorophyll and other undesirable plant compounds, which may require additional post-processing to refine the final product.

2. **Benefits and drawbacks of solvent-based extraction**

Benefits of solvent-based extraction include:

- **Efficiency**: Solvent-based extraction methods are highly efficient at extracting cannabinoids and terpenes from cannabis plant material, resulting in a potent and concentrated final product.

- **Versatility**: Solvent-based extraction methods can be used to create a variety of cannabis concentrates, including shatter, wax, and crumble, depending on the specific techniques and conditions used during the process.

- **Scalability**: Solvent-based extraction methods can be easily scaled up for large-scale production, making them suitable for commercial cannabis operations.

Drawbacks of solvent-based extraction include:

- **Safety concerns**: The use of flammable solvents, such as butane and propane, can pose significant safety risks during the extraction process if not handled properly. This includes the risk of explosion, fire, and exposure to harmful fumes.

- **Residual solvents**: If not properly purged, residual solvents can remain in the final product, potentially posing health risks to consumers.

- **Complexity**: Solvent-based extraction methods often require specialized equipment and skilled operators to ensure a safe and efficient process.

3. Safety concerns and best practices

When performing solvent-based extraction, it is crucial to prioritize safety and adhere to best practices, including:

- **Proper ventilation**: Ensure that the extraction area is well-ventilated to prevent the buildup of flammable fumes.

- **Use of closed-loop systems**: Closed-loop extraction systems help to minimize the risk of solvent leaks and exposure to harmful fumes by containing the solvent within a closed system.

- **Proper purging**: Use heat and vacuum to remove residual solvents from the final product, ensuring a safe and clean concentrate.

- **Operator training**: Ensure that extraction operators are trained in the safe handling of solvents and the proper operation of extraction equipment.

By following these best practices, solvent-based extraction can be a safe and effective method for producing high-quality cannabis concentrates and products.

CO2 Extraction

CO2 extraction is a popular and advanced method for extracting cannabinoids and terpenes from cannabis plant material. This method uses carbon dioxide (CO2) as a solvent, which offers several benefits over traditional solvent-based extraction methods. CO2 extraction is known for its efficiency, purity, and ability to produce high-quality extracts with minimal post-processing.

There are two primary types of CO2 extraction: supercritical and subcritical. Both methods use CO2 as the solvent but operate under different temperature and pressure conditions, resulting in extracts with different properties.

1. **Supercritical and Subcritical CO2 Extraction**

    - **Supercritical CO2 extraction**: This method uses CO2 in its supercritical state, which means it exhibits properties of both a liquid and a gas. Supercritical CO2 extraction operates at higher temperatures and pressures, allowing for a more efficient and faster extraction process. However, higher temperatures can sometimes cause the degradation of heat-sensitive terpenes, altering the flavor and aroma of the final product.

- **Subcritical CO_2 extraction**: This method uses CO_2 in its liquid state, operating at lower temperatures and pressures compared to supercritical extraction. Subcritical CO_2 extraction preserves heat-sensitive terpenes and other volatile compounds, resulting in a more flavorful and aromatic extract. However, this method is generally slower and less efficient than supercritical extraction, which can increase production costs and time.

2. Benefits and Drawbacks of CO_2 Extraction

Benefits of CO_2 extraction include:

- **Purity**: CO_2 extraction produces a high-quality extract with minimal impurities and no residual solvents, making it ideal for producing medical-grade cannabis products.

- **Selectivity**: By adjusting temperature and pressure, CO_2 extraction can be fine-tuned to target specific cannabinoids and terpenes, creating customized extracts.

- **Environmentally friendly**: CO_2 is a naturally occurring, non-toxic solvent that can be easily recovered and reused during extraction, reducing waste and environmental impact.

- **Scalability**: CO_2 extraction can be scaled up for large-scale production, making it suitable for commercial cannabis operations.

Drawbacks of CO_2 extraction include:

- **High initial investment**: CO_2 extraction requires specialized equipment and infrastructure, which can be expensive to purchase and maintain.

- **Complexity**: CO_2 extraction involves a complex process that requires skilled operators and precise control over temperature and pressure to achieve optimal results.

3. Equipment and Operational Requirements

CO_2 extraction requires specialized equipment and infrastructure, such as:

- **CO_2 extraction system**: A closed-loop extraction system designed to contain and control CO_2 throughout the extraction process.

- **Temperature and pressure control units**: Devices that regulate the temperature and pressure within the extraction system to achieve the desired extraction conditions.

- **CO_2 recovery system**: This recovers and recycles CO_2 during extraction, reducing waste and operational costs.

- **Post-processing equipment**: Depending on the desired final product, additional equipment may be required for post-processing, such as winterization, decarboxylation, or fractional distillation.

Operators of CO_2 extraction equipment should be trained in the proper operation, maintenance, and safety procedures to ensure a safe and efficient extraction process.

By understanding and properly implementing CO_2 extraction techniques, cannabis manufacturers can produce high-quality, pure, and customized extracts for a variety of applications.

Rosin Pressing

Rosin pressing is a solventless extraction method that uses heat and pressure to extract cannabinoids and terpenes from cannabis plant material. This method is gaining popularity due to its simplicity, safety, and ability to produce a high-quality concentrate without the use of potentially harmful solvents.

The rosin pressing process involves placing cannabis plant material, such as flower or kief, between two heated plates. Pressure is then applied, forcing the cannabinoids and terpenes to melt and separate from the plant material. The resulting liquid, called rosin, is collected and allowed to cool, resulting in a pure and potent concentrate.

1. Equipment and Materials

Rosin pressing requires relatively simple equipment and materials, including:

- **Rosin press:** A device specifically designed to apply heat and pressure to cannabis plant material. Rosin presses can range from manual models to more advanced hydraulic or pneumatic models with precise temperature and pressure controls.

- **Pressing plates**: The heated surfaces that come into contact with the cannabis plant material during the rosin pressing process. These plates should be made of materials that can withstand high temperatures and pressure, such as stainless steel or aluminum.

- **Parchment paper or non-stick sheets**: Used to collect the rosin as it is pressed from the plant material, ensuring that the concentrate does not stick to the pressing plates or other surfaces.

- **Cannabis plant material**: High-quality cannabis flower, kief, or bubble hash can be used as the starting material for rosin pressing. The quality of the plant material will directly affect the quality, potency, and yield of the final rosin product.

2. Tips for Optimizing Rosin Pressing

To achieve the best results when pressing rosin, consider the following tips:

- **Start with high-quality plant material**: The quality and potency of the cannabis flower, kief, or hash used will directly influence the final rosin product

- **Control temperature and pressure**: Experiment with different temperature and pressure settings to find the optimal conditions to extract the highest yield and quality of rosin from your specific plant material.

- **Pre-press the plant material**: Using a pre-press mold to compact the cannabis plant material before pressing can help to improve the efficiency and overall yield of the rosin pressing process.

- **Monitor pressing time**: The duration of the pressing process can also impact the quality and yield of the rosin. Adjust the pressing time as needed to achieve the desired results.

By understanding the rosin pressing process and optimizing the extraction conditions, cannabis producers can create high-quality, solvent-free concentrates for various applications.

Cold Water Extraction (Bubble Hash)

Cold water extraction, also known as bubble hash or ice water extraction, is a solventless method for extracting cannabinoids, terpenes, and other compounds from cannabis plant material.

Cold water extraction involves mixing cannabis plant material with cold water and ice. The low temperature of the water causes the trichomes, which house the cannabinoids and terpenes, to become brittle and break off from the plant material. The mixture is then agitated either manually or mechanically to encourage the separation of the trichomes. The resulting mixture is then filtered through a series of mesh bags or screens to collect the trichomes, which can be dried and pressed into bubble hash.

1. Equipment and Materials

To perform cold water extraction, you will need the following equipment and materials:

- **Cold water**: Cold water is essential for making the trichomes brittle and facilitating their separation from the plant material.

- **Ice**: Adding ice to the water helps to maintain a low temperature throughout the extraction process.

- **Cannabis plant material**: High-quality cannabis flower or trim can be used as the starting material for cold water extraction. The quality of the plant material will directly affect the quality, potency, and yield of the final bubble hash product.

- **Mixing container**: A large container, such as a bucket or a washing machine specifically designed for cold water extraction, is needed for mixing the cannabis plant material with cold water and ice.

- **Mesh bags or screens**: A set of mesh bags or screens with varying micron sizes is required for filtering the trichomes from the water mixture. These bags or screens are often called "bubble bags."

- **Spatula or scraper**: A tool for collecting the trichomes from the mesh bags or screens after filtering.

Dry Sift Extraction

Dry sift extraction is a solventless method for separating trichomes from cannabis plant material to produce a potent and pure concentrate.

The dry sift extraction process involves agitating dried cannabis plant material over a series of mesh screens or silk screens with varying micron sizes. The agitation causes the trichomes to break away from the plant material and fall through the screens. By using screens with different micron sizes, smaller trichomes can be separated from larger plant particles, resulting in a fine, powdery concentrate known as dry sift or kief.

1. Equipment and Materials

To perform dry sift extraction, you will need the following equipment and materials:

- **Cannabis plant material**: High-quality cannabis flower or trim can be used as the starting material for dry sift extraction. The quality of the plant material will directly affect the quality, potency, and yield of the final dry-sift product.

- **Drying and curing**: You can refer to the previous chapter on this method. Properly dried and cured cannabis plant material allows for easier trichome separation and improved flavor and aroma in the final product.

- **Mesh screens or silk screens**: A set of mesh or silk screens with varying micron sizes is required for filtering the trichomes from the plant material. The screens are often stacked or arranged in a box-like structure called a dry sift box or pollen box.

- **Agitating tools**: Tools or devices for gently agitating the plant material over the screens, such as a card, brush, or an automated tumbler.

Supercritical CO2 Extraction

Supercritical CO_2 extraction is a highly efficient and advanced method for extracting cannabinoids, terpenes, and other compounds from cannabis plant material.

The supercritical CO_2 extraction process involves passing CO_2 through a closed-loop system containing cannabis plant material. The CO_2 is heated and pressurized to reach its supercritical state, which allows it to act as a solvent and extract the cannabinoids, terpenes, and other compounds from the plant material. The CO_2 and extracted compounds are then separated in a collection chamber, and the CO_2 is either recycled or released, leaving behind a high-quality, pure concentrate.

1. Equipment and Materials

Supercritical CO_2 extraction requires specialized equipment and materials, including:

- **CO_2 extraction machine**: A closed-loop system specifically designed for supercritical CO_2 extraction. These machines can vary in size and complexity, with some models designed for small-scale operations and others for large-scale production.

- **Carbon dioxide (CO_2):** High-purity CO_2 is used as the solvent for extracting the desired compounds from the cannabis plant material.

- **Cannabis plant material**: High-quality cannabis flower or trim can be used as the starting material for supercritical CO_2 extraction. The quality of the plant material will directly affect the quality, potency, and yield of the final concentrate product.

Ethanol Extraction

Ethanol extraction is a popular method for extracting cannabinoids, terpenes, and other compounds from cannabis plant material.

The ethanol extraction process involves soaking or washing cannabis plant material in ethanol, which dissolves the cannabinoids, terpenes, and other compounds from the plant. The ethanol and extracted compounds are then separated from the plant material through filtration or centrifugation. The ethanol is evaporated, leaving behind a concentrated cannabis extract. This extract can be further refined through additional processing steps, such as winterization and distillation, to improve its purity and potency.

1. Equipment and Materials

Ethanol extraction requires specific equipment and materials, including:

- **Ethanol**: High-purity, food-grade ethanol is used as the solvent for extracting the desired compounds from the cannabis plant material. Denatured ethanol, which contains additives to make it unfit for human consumption, should not be used for extraction.

- **Cannabis plant material**: High-quality cannabis flower or trim can be used as the starting material for ethanol extraction. The quality of the plant material will directly affect the quality, potency, and yield of the final concentrate product.

- **Extraction vessel**: A container, such as a glass jar or stainless-steel vessel, is needed for soaking or washing the cannabis plant material in ethanol.

- **Filtration or centrifugation equipment**: Equipment for separating the ethanol and extracted compounds from the plant material, such as a vacuum-assisted filtration system or a centrifuge.

- **Evaporation equipment**: A rotary evaporator, vacuum oven, or similar device is required for evaporating the ethanol and recovering the concentrated cannabis extract.

2. Benefits and Drawbacks of Ethanol Extraction

Benefits of ethanol extraction include:

- **Safety**: Ethanol is a non-toxic, non-flammable solvent that is generally recognized as safe (GRAS) for use in food and pharmaceutical products.

- **Efficiency**: Ethanol extraction is highly efficient and can yield large amounts of concentrate from cannabis plant material.

- **Simplicity**: Ethanol extraction is relatively simple and does not require specialized knowledge or advanced equipment, making it accessible to small-scale cannabis producers and home growers.

- **Purity**: To improve its purity and potency, the final concentrate produced through ethanol extraction can be further refined through additional processing steps, such as winterization and distillation.

Drawbacks of ethanol extraction include:

- **Solubility of undesired compounds**: Ethanol can also dissolve chlorophyll and other unwanted compounds from the cannabis plant material, which may need to be removed through additional processing steps.

- **Evaporation**: The ethanol must be evaporated and recovered after extraction, which can be time-consuming and requires specialized equipment.

- **Flammability**: Although ethanol is considered non-toxic, it is still flammable and should be handled with caution.

3. Tips for Optimizing Ethanol Extraction

To achieve the best results when performing ethanol extraction, consider the following tips:

- **Start with high-quality plant material**: The quality and potency of the cannabis flower or trim used will directly influence the final concentrate product.

- **Use high-purity ethanol**: Ensure that you use high-purity, food-grade ethanol for extraction to prevent contamination and ensure a high-quality final product.

- **Control temperature**: Adjusting the temperature during the extraction process can help to minimize the solubility of undesired compounds, such as chlorophyll, in ethanol. Lower temperatures (e.g., -20°C to -40°C) are often used for this purpose.

- **Perform additional processing steps**: Refine the extracted concentrate through additional processing steps, such as winterization and distillation, to improve its purity and potency

By understanding the ethanol extraction process and following these tips, cannabis producers can create high-quality, pure concentrates for various applications.

Hydrocarbon Extraction

Hydrocarbon extraction is a widely used method for extracting cannabinoids, terpenes, and other compounds from cannabis plant material.

The hydrocarbon extraction process involves passing a hydrocarbon solvent, such as butane or propane, through a closed-loop system containing cannabis plant material. The solvent dissolves the cannabinoids, terpenes, and other compounds from the plant material. The solvent and extracted compounds are then separated from the plant material and collected in a collection chamber. The solvent is evaporated, leaving behind a concentrated cannabis extract commonly known as butane hash oil (BHO) or propane hash oil (PHO), depending on the solvent used.

1. Equipment and Materials

Hydrocarbon extraction requires specialized equipment and materials, including:

- **Closed-loop extraction system**: A closed-loop system specifically designed for hydrocarbon extraction is required. These systems can vary in size and complexity, with some models designed for small-scale operations and others for large-scale production.

- **Hydrocarbon solvent**: High-purity butane, propane, or a mix of both can be used to extract the desired compounds from the cannabis plant material.

- **Cannabis plant material**: High-quality cannabis flower or trim can be used as the starting material for hydrocarbon extraction. The quality of the plant material will directly affect the quality, potency, and yield of the final concentrate product.

- **Evaporation equipment**: A vacuum oven or similar device is required for evaporating the solvent and recovering the concentrated cannabis extract.

Production of Concentrates and Oils

Cannabis concentrates and oils are highly potent forms of cannabis, containing high concentrations of cannabinoids and terpenes.

These products are derived from the cannabis plant through various extraction processes, which aim to isolate and extract the desired compounds while leaving behind the plant material.

There are various types of cannabis concentrates, including:

- **Shatter**: A glass-like, translucent concentrate that is brittle and can shatter when dropped or manipulated. Shatter has a high potency and is often consumed through dabbing.

- **Wax**: A soft, opaque concentrate with a texture similar to wax. It is more pliable than shatter and can be consumed through dabbing or vaporization.

- **Crumble**: A crumbly, honeycomb-like concentrate that can be broken apart easily. Crumble is often consumed through dabbing or vaporization.

- **Budder**: A creamy, butter-like concentrate that is soft and easy to spread. Budder can be consumed through dabbing, vaporization, or as an ingredient in edibles.

Cannabis oils come in various forms, including:

- **Distillate**: A highly refined oil that contains a high concentration of a single cannabinoid, such as THC or CBD. Distillates are often used in vape cartridges, edibles, and tinctures.

- **Full-spectrum**: An oil that contains a wide range of cannabinoids, terpenes, and other compounds found in the cannabis plant. Full-spectrum oils aim to preserve the plant's natural profile and are believed to provide an "entourage effect" due to the synergistic interactions between the various compounds.

Consumption Methods and Devices

Cannabis concentrates and oils can be consumed in several ways, including:

- **Dabbing**: A method of consuming concentrates by heating a small amount on a heated surface (called a "nail" or "banger") and inhaling the vapor through a specialized glass piece known as a dab rig.

- **Vaporizers**: Devices that heat concentrates or oils to a specific temperature to produce vapor that is inhaled. Vaporizers come in various forms, such as vape pens, portable vaporizers, and desktop vaporizers.

- **Tinctures**: Concentrates and oils can be mixed with a carrier oil or alcohol to create tinctures, which can be consumed orally or sublingually (under the tongue).

- **Edibles**: Concentrates and oils can be infused into various food and beverage products, such as baked goods, gummies, and chocolates.

Production of Tinctures

Cannabis tinctures are liquid extracts of cannabinoids and terpenes, typically made by dissolving cannabis concentrates or plant material in a carrier liquid such as alcohol or oil. Tinctures can be consumed orally or sublingually, offering a discreet, easy-to-dose consumption method.

- **Alcohol-based tinctures**: These tinctures use high-proof alcohol as the carrier liquid, which acts as a solvent to extract the desired compounds from the cannabis plant material or concentrate. Alcohol-based tinctures have a long shelf life and can be consumed directly or mixed with food or beverages.

- **Oil-based tinctures**: These tinctures use a carrier oil, such as MCT oil or olive oil, to dissolve the cannabis concentrate or plant material. Oil-based tinctures have a milder taste compared to alcohol-based tinctures and can be consumed directly or mixed with food or beverages.

Methods for Making Tinctures at Home

- **Cold maceration**: This method involves soaking cannabis plant material in a high-proof alcohol or carrier oil for an extended period (typically several weeks) in a cool, dark place. The mixture is periodically shaken to help extract the desired compounds.

- **Warm maceration**: Similar to cold maceration, but the mixture is gently heated (e.g., in a slow cooker or double boiler) to speed up the extraction process. The mixture is then strained and bottled for consumption.

Dosage: Tincture potency can vary widely depending on the cannabis concentrate or plant material used and the extraction method. Start with a low dose (e.g., 1-2 drops) and gradually increase to find the optimal dosage for your needs.

Consumption methods: Tinctures can be consumed orally, sublingually (absorbed under the tongue), or mixed with food or beverages.

Production of Edibles

Cannabis edibles are food and beverage products infused with cannabinoids, terpenes, and other compounds extracted from the cannabis plant. Edibles offer a discreet and convenient consumption method, with effects that typically last longer compared to inhalation methods.

There are various types of cannabis edibles, including:

- **Baked goods**: Brownies, cookies, and other baked goods are common forms of cannabis edibles. They are typically infused with cannabis butter or oil.

- **Gummies**: Cannabis-infused gummy candies are a popular edible option due to their convenience, portability, and precise dosing.

- **Beverages**: Cannabis-infused beverages, such as teas, sodas, and juices, offer an alternative way to consume cannabis edibles.

Cannabis can be infused into several ingredients to create edibles, including:

- **Cannabutter**: Butter infused with cannabis, often used in baked goods. Cannabutter is made by gently heating cannabis plant material with butter to extract the desired compounds.

- **Cannabis oil**: Cannabis-infused oil, such as coconut or olive oil, can be used in various recipes. Cannabis oil is made by heating cannabis plant material with the carrier oil to extract the desired compounds.

Dosage: Edibles can vary widely in potency depending on the cannabis-infused ingredient used and the recipe. Start with a low dose (e.g., 5-10 mg of THC) and wait at least 1-2 hours before consuming more to gauge the effects.

Consumption methods: Edibles can be consumed directly or incorporated into various recipes. Always consume edibles responsibly and be aware that their effects may take longer to onset compared to inhalation methods.

Production of Topicals

Cannabis topicals are creams, balms, salves, and other products infused with cannabinoids and terpenes that are applied directly to the skin. Topicals offer localized relief and are typically non-psychoactive, making them a popular option for those seeking the therapeutic benefits of cannabis without the intoxicating effects.

Cannabis topicals come in various forms, including:

- **Creams**: Cannabis-infused creams have a smooth, lotion-like consistency and are often used for moisturizing and soothing the skin.

- **Balms**: Cannabis-infused balms have a thicker, waxier consistency and are typically used for targeted relief of sore muscles and joints.

- **Salves**: Cannabis-infused salves are similar to balms but have a softer consistency and are often used for minor skin irritations and inflammation.

Cannabis topicals offer several benefits, including:

- **Localized relief**: Topicals provide targeted relief for a variety of skin conditions, muscle aches, and joint pain.

- **Non-psychoactive**: Unlike other consumption methods, topicals typically do not produce intoxicating effects, making them suitable for those seeking the therapeutic benefits of cannabis without the "high."

Dosage: Topicals can vary in potency depending on the cannabis-infused ingredient used and the formulation. Start with a small amount and apply more as needed to achieve the desired level of relief.

Application methods: Apply cannabis topicals directly to the affected area and massage into the skin until fully absorbed. Reapply as needed for continued relief.

Chapter 9: Medicinal and Therapeutic Uses of Cannabis

Cannabis has been used for its medicinal properties for thousands of years, with historical records dating back to ancient China, Egypt, and Greece. In recent years, interest in the therapeutic potential of cannabis has grown significantly, fueled by changing attitudes toward the plant, anecdotal evidence, and an increasing body of scientific research.

9. Forms of medicinal cannabis. Source: BruceBlaus. When using this image in external sources it can be cited as: Blausen.com staff (2014). "Medical gallery of Blausen Medical 2014". WikiJournal of Medicine 1 (2). DOI:10.15347/wjm/2014.010. ISSN 2002-4436., CC BY 3.0 <https://creativecommons.org/licenses/by/3.0>, via Wikimedia Commons: https://commons.wikimedia.org/wiki/File:Blausen_0158_Cannabis_Medicina l.png

Cannabinoids, Terpenes, and the Endocannabinoid System

Cannabinoids are a diverse group of chemical compounds found in the cannabis plant, with delta-9-tetrahydrocannabinol (THC) and cannabidiol (CBD) being the most well-known and studied. THC is the primary psychoactive component, responsible for the characteristic "high" associated with cannabis use, while CBD is non-psychoactive and has been studied for its potential therapeutic benefits.

Terpenes are volatile organic compounds found in the essential oils of plants, including cannabis. They are responsible for the plant's aroma and flavor and have been studied for their potential health benefits, including anti-inflammatory, analgesic, and anxiolytic properties.

The endocannabinoid system (ECS) is a complex cell-signaling system found throughout the human body, playing a crucial role in maintaining homeostasis. It is composed of endocannabinoids (naturally occurring compounds similar to plant-derived cannabinoids), receptors (CB1 and CB2), and enzymes responsible for their synthesis and degradation. The ECS regulates a wide range of physiological processes, including immune response, pain sensation, mood, memory, and sleep.

Cannabinoids and terpenes in cannabis interact with the ECS, modulating its activity and potentially providing therapeutic benefits. For example, THC binds primarily to CB1 receptors, producing its psychoactive effects, while CBD has a lower affinity for these receptors and may indirectly influence their activity.

Treating Various Conditions and Symptoms with Cannabis

1. Chronic Pain Management

Cannabis has been widely studied for its analgesic properties. Research indicates that cannabinoids, particularly THC and CBD, may help alleviate various types of chronic pain, including neuropathic pain, inflammatory pain, and cancer-related pain. The modulation of the ECS and interaction with other neurotransmitter systems are believed to contribute to these effects.

2. Anxiety and Stress Relief

Cannabis, particularly CBD, has shown the potential to reduce anxiety and stress. Research suggests that CBD may help alleviate symptoms of generalized anxiety disorder, social anxiety disorder, and post-traumatic stress disorder (PTSD). The anxiolytic effects are thought to be mediated by interactions with serotonin receptors and modulation of the ECS.

3. Insomnia and Sleep Disorders

Cannabis has been used for centuries to promote sleep and relaxation. Research indicates that cannabinoids, particularly THC and CBD, may improve sleep quality and duration in individuals who have insomnia and other sleep disorders. These effects may be attributed to the sedative properties of THC and the anxiolytic and anti-inflammatory properties of CBD.

4. Epilepsy and Seizure Control

Cannabis, specifically CBD, has gained attention for its potential to reduce the frequency and severity of seizures in patients with epilepsy, including treatment-resistant forms such as Dravet syndrome and Lennox-Gastaut syndrome. The FDA has approved a CBD-based medication, Epidiolex, for these conditions, highlighting the growing acceptance of cannabis as a viable treatment option.

5. Nausea and Vomiting

Cannabis has been used to alleviate nausea and vomiting associated with chemotherapy and other medical treatments. Research suggests that THC is particularly effective in reducing these symptoms by activating CB1 receptors in the brain and gastrointestinal tract.

6. Other Potential Therapeutic Applications

Cannabis has been studied for a variety of other conditions, including multiple sclerosis (MS), glaucoma, and inflammatory bowel disease (IBD). While more research is needed, preliminary findings suggest potential benefits in reducing spasticity, intraocular pressure, and inflammation.

Consumption Methods and Their Implications for Medicinal Use

There are several ways to consume cannabis for medicinal purposes, each with its advantages and disadvantages:

- **Inhalation methods (smoking, vaporization):** Rapid onset of effects, easy dose titration, and relatively high bioavailability. However, potential respiratory risks are associated with smoking, and both methods may not be suitable for patients with respiratory issues.

- **Oral consumption (edibles, tinctures, capsules):** Longer-lasting effects, discreet, and no respiratory risks. However, drawbacks include delayed onset, variable absorption, and the potential for overconsumption.

- **Topical application (creams, balms, salves):** Localized relief for skin conditions, inflammation, and pain. However, there is the risk of limited systemic absorption and lower bioavailability.

- **Sublingual administration (tinctures, sprays, strips):** Rapid onset, high bioavailability, and discreet. However, there is the potential for variable absorption and limited product availability.

- **Suppositories**: Rapid absorption and high bioavailability, suitable for patients unable to consume cannabis orally. However, there is the potential for discomfort and limited product availability

Dosing Considerations for Medicinal Cannabis

Proper dosing and titration are crucial for achieving optimal therapeutic benefits while minimizing side effects. Factors influencing dosage include age, weight, tolerance, the specific condition being treated, and individual metabolism.

A common approach is to start with a low dose and gradually increase it until the desired effects are achieved, maintaining a balance between therapeutic benefits and potential side effects. Consultation with a healthcare professional experienced in cannabis therapy is recommended for personalized guidance.

Short-term side effects of cannabis use may include dizziness, dry mouth, fatigue, and increased heart rate. Long-term risks include dependence, cognitive impairment, and respiratory issues (particularly with smoking). Cannabis may interact with other medications and may be contraindicated in certain health conditions, such as a history of psychosis or cardiovascular disease.

The medicinal and therapeutic potential of cannabis continues to gain recognition as research advances and societal attitudes evolve. The growing acceptance of cannabis as a viable treatment option for various conditions and symptoms highlights the importance of continued research and education in this field. Individualized approaches to cannabis therapy and patient care are crucial for optimizing outcomes while minimizing risks. As our understanding of cannabis and its interactions with the human body deepens, so too will our ability to harness its potential for the benefit of patients in need.

Chapter 10: Responsible Cultivation and Legal Considerations

As the legal landscape surrounding cannabis continues to evolve, cultivators must prioritize responsible and sustainable practices. This includes adhering to local laws and regulations governing the production, distribution, and consumption of cannabis and implementing environmentally friendly cultivation methods. By promoting a sustainable and safe cannabis industry, cultivators can contribute to the long-term success of this burgeoning sector and foster greater acceptance within society.

■ Both medical and recreational use legal
■ Medical use legal, recreational use decriminalized
■ Medical use legal, recreational use illegal, but law is often unenforced
■ Medical and recreational use illegal
■ Both medical and recreational use decriminalized
■ Both medical and recreational use illegal, but law is often unenforced
■ Both medical and recreational use illegal
■ No information

10. *World map of cannabis legality per country. Source: Povke19991211, CC0, via Wikimedia Commons:*
https://commons.wikimedia.org/wiki/File:Legality_of_cannabis_by_country. PNG

The Importance of Adhering to Local Laws and Regulations

Compliance with local laws and regulations is essential for the legitimacy and stability of the cannabis industry. These regulations are designed to ensure the safety of consumers, protect public health, and prevent the diversion of products to the illicit market. Failure to adhere to these rules can result in significant legal consequences for cultivators, including fines, license revocation, and even criminal charges.

Moreover, compliance with regulations helps to build trust with consumers, local communities, and regulators. By demonstrating a commitment to operating within the bounds of the law, cultivators can set a positive example for others in the industry and contribute to the ongoing normalization of cannabis as a legitimate and valuable commodity.

Responsible cultivation practices not only benefit the environment but also contribute to the overall safety and sustainability of the cannabis industry. By adopting eco-friendly methods such as water conservation, energy efficiency, and waste reduction, cultivators can minimize their environmental impact and promote the long-term viability of cannabis production.

In addition, responsible cultivation entails ensuring the safety and well-being of those who come into contact with cannabis products. This includes preventing unauthorized access to cannabis plants and products, particularly by children and other vulnerable populations, and implementing rigorous quality control measures to guarantee the purity and potency of cannabis products.

By embracing responsible cultivation practices, cultivators play a crucial role in shaping the future of the cannabis industry. Their commitment to sustainability, safety, and compliance with local laws and regulations sets the stage for a thriving and socially responsible sector that benefits both consumers and the wider community.

To ensure compliance with local laws and regulations, cultivators must familiarize themselves with the various requirements and restrictions governing cannabis cultivation in their jurisdiction. This includes understanding the licensing process, restrictions on possession and distribution, zoning and land use regulations, and compliance with state and federal regulations pertaining to pesticides and worker safety.

Licensing Requirements and Application Processes

In many jurisdictions, individuals and businesses must obtain a license or permit to cultivate cannabis legally. Licensing requirements vary by jurisdiction and may include background checks, proof of financial stability, demonstration of cultivation expertise, and a detailed business plan. The application process often involves submitting an application form, paying applicable fees, and providing documentation to support the application.

Prospective cultivators must familiarize themselves with their jurisdiction's licensing requirements and application processes to increase their chances of obtaining the necessary approvals. This may involve consulting with legal and industry professionals or attending workshops and informational sessions hosted by regulatory agencies.

Laws and regulations governing the possession, distribution, and sale of cannabis vary significantly by jurisdiction and can directly impact how cultivators operate their businesses. For example, some jurisdictions may impose limits on the number of plants that can be cultivated or the amount of cannabis that can be possessed or sold. Others may restrict the types of cannabis products that can be produced or sold, such as edibles, concentrates, or topicals.

Cultivators must be aware of these restrictions and ensure that their operations are in compliance with all applicable laws and regulations to avoid potential legal consequences.

Zoning and Land Use Regulations

Cannabis cultivation is subject to zoning and land use regulations, which dictate where and how cultivation facilities can be established and operated. These regulations may restrict cultivation to specific zones or require cultivators to maintain a certain distance from sensitive areas such as schools, parks, or residential neighborhoods. In addition, local governments may impose requirements related to building codes, fire safety, and environmental protection.

To ensure compliance with zoning and land use regulations, cultivators should consult with local planning and zoning officials and obtain any necessary permits or approvals before establishing their cultivation facilities.

Cannabis cultivators must also comply with state and federal regulations concerning the use of pesticides, worker safety, and other matters. For example, cultivators may need to adhere to specific guidelines regarding the types of pesticides that can be used on cannabis plants and the proper storage and disposal of these chemicals. In addition, cultivators must ensure that their operations comply with worker safety regulations, such as providing appropriate protective equipment and training for employees and maintaining safe working conditions.

Compliance with these regulations not only protects the health and safety of workers and consumers but also helps to maintain the legitimacy and credibility of the cannabis industry as a whole. By staying informed about regulatory requirements and proactively implementing best practices, cultivators can contribute to a safe, sustainable, and responsible cannabis sector.

Sustainable and Eco-Friendly Cultivation Practices

Adopting sustainable and eco-friendly cultivation practices is crucial for minimizing the environmental impact of cannabis production and promoting the industry's long-term viability. By implementing measures to conserve water, reduce energy consumption, manage pests responsibly, and minimize waste, cultivators can contribute to a greener and more sustainable cannabis sector.

Water Conservation and Efficient Irrigation Techniques

Cannabis cultivation can be water-intensive, making it essential for cultivators to adopt water conservation practices and efficient irrigation techniques. Some strategies to conserve water in cannabis cultivation include:

1. Using drip irrigation systems to deliver water directly to the plant roots, minimizing water waste through evaporation or runoff.

2. Implementing moisture sensors and automated irrigation systems to monitor soil moisture levels and apply water only when necessary.

3. Collecting rainwater or using greywater for irrigation, reducing reliance on freshwater sources.

4. Selecting drought-tolerant cannabis strains that require less water to grow.

5. Energy efficiency measures (e.g., LED lighting, solar power)

Cannabis cultivation, particularly in indoor facilities, can consume significant amounts of energy for lighting, climate control, and other systems. To reduce energy consumption and greenhouse gas emissions, cultivators can implement energy efficiency measures such as:

1. Installing energy-efficient LED lighting consumes less energy and generates less heat than traditional HID lamps.

2. Utilizing solar panels or other renewable energy sources to power cultivation facilities reduces reliance on fossil fuels.

3. Insulating and sealing cultivation facilities to minimize heat loss and reduce energy consumption for heating and cooling.

4. Implementing energy management systems to monitor and optimize energy use in real-time.

Integrated Pest Management and Organic Cultivation Methods

Pest management is a critical aspect of cannabis cultivation, but the use of synthetic pesticides can harm the environment and pose risks to human health. Integrated pest management (IPM) is an eco-friendly approach to pest control that focuses on prevention, monitoring, and the use of least-toxic control methods. Some IPM strategies for cannabis cultivation include:

1. Regularly monitoring plants for signs of pests or disease and implementing targeted controls when necessary.

2. Encouraging the presence of beneficial insects and predators to help control pests naturally.

3. Using organic or least-toxic pesticides ensures they are applied per label instructions and local regulations.

4. Maintaining a clean and healthy cultivation environment to minimize the risk of pest infestations.

Waste Management and Recycling Initiatives

Effective waste management and recycling practices are essential for reducing the environmental impact of cannabis cultivation. Some strategies for managing waste and promoting recycling in cultivation operations include:

1. Composting plant waste such as leaves, stems, and root balls, returns valuable nutrients to the soil and reduces the need for synthetic fertilizers.

2. Reusing or recycling containers, pots, and other cultivation materials, minimizing the consumption of new resources.

3. Properly disposing of hazardous waste, such as used pesticides or nutrient solutions, in accordance with local regulations.

4. Implementing waste reduction initiatives, such as reducing packaging materials or encouraging customers to return used containers for recycling or reuse.

By adopting these sustainable and eco-friendly cultivation practices, cannabis cultivators can minimize their environmental impact, promote the industry's long-term viability, and contribute to a more responsible and sustainable cannabis sector.

Safe Storage and Preventing Unauthorized Access

Ensuring the safe storage of cannabis and related products is essential for protecting public health, preventing unauthorized access, and reducing the risk of theft and diversion to the illicit market. Cultivators must implement a variety of measures to secure their products and protect vulnerable populations, such as children, pets, and others who may be at risk.

Proper storage of cannabis and related products (e.g., locked containers, climate control)

Proper storage of cannabis and related products is crucial for maintaining product quality, potency, and safety. Some best practices for storing cannabis and related products include:

1. Storing cannabis products in locked containers or secure storage areas that are inaccessible to unauthorized individuals.

2. Utilizing climate-controlled storage solutions to maintain optimal temperature and humidity levels can help preserve the potency and freshness of cannabis products.

3. Keeping cannabis products separate from other items, such as food or medications, to prevent contamination or accidental ingestion.

4. Labeling cannabis products clearly and accurately, including information about strain, potency, and any applicable warnings or usage instructions.

Measures to Prevent Theft and Diversion to the Illicit Market

Cultivators must take steps to prevent theft and diversion of cannabis products to the illicit market, which can undermine the legitimacy of the legal cannabis industry and pose risks to public health and safety. Some strategies for preventing theft and diversion include:

1. Implementing robust security measures at cultivation facilities, such as surveillance cameras, access controls, and alarm systems.

2. Conducting thorough background checks on employees and contractors to minimize the risk of insider theft or collusion.

3. Maintaining accurate inventory records and tracking systems to monitor the movement of cannabis products throughout the supply chain.

4. Establishing clear policies and procedures for reporting suspected theft, diversion, or other security

incidents and training employees to recognize and respond to potential threats.

Ensuring the Safety of Children, Pets, and Other Vulnerable Populations

Cannabis cultivators are responsible for protecting vulnerable populations, such as children and pets, from potential exposure to cannabis products. This includes implementing storage and packaging measures to reduce the risk of accidental ingestion or exposure. Some strategies for protecting vulnerable populations include:

1. Designing child-resistant packaging for cannabis products to deter access by young children.

2. Using clear and prominent warning labels on cannabis products to alert caregivers and consumers to the potential risks associated with ingestion or exposure.

3. Educating employees, customers, and the wider community about the importance of safe storage and responsible cannabis use, particularly around children and pets.

4. Collaborating with public health organizations, schools, and other stakeholders to develop and disseminate educational materials and resources related to cannabis safety.

By prioritizing safe storage and preventing unauthorized access, cultivators can contribute to a safer and more responsible cannabis industry that protects vulnerable populations and discourages illicit market activity.

Responsible Community Engagement and Education

Cannabis cultivators have an important role to play in fostering responsible community engagement and education. By actively engaging with their local communities, cultivators can help build positive relationships with neighbors, local stakeholders, and consumers, promote responsible cannabis use, and contribute to the community's overall well-being. The following strategies can help cultivators achieve these goals:

Building Positive Relationships with Neighbors and Local Stakeholders

Establishing and maintaining open lines of communication with neighbors and local stakeholders is essential for building trust and ensuring a positive relationship between cannabis cultivators and the surrounding community. Some ways to build positive relationships include:

1. Organizing community meetings and open houses to provide information about the cultivation facility and its operations and addressing concerns or questions from community members.

2. Participating in local events, such as community fairs, farmer's markets, or neighborhood gatherings, to foster positive interactions with community members and demonstrate a commitment to local engagement.

3. Collaborating with local law enforcement, regulators, and other stakeholders to ensure compliance with regulations and address any public safety concerns.

Educating the Community about the Benefits and Risks of Cannabis Use

Cultivators have a unique opportunity to educate the community about the potential benefits and risks associated with cannabis use. By providing accurate, evidence-based information, cultivators can help dispel myths and misconceptions about cannabis and promote informed decision-making among consumers. Some strategies for educating the community include:

1. Hosting educational events, seminars, or workshops on topics related to cannabis cultivation, consumption, and safety.

2. Developing and distributing educational materials, such as pamphlets, posters, or online resources that provide accurate and accessible information about cannabis use, benefits, and risks.

3. Collaborating with healthcare professionals, researchers, and other experts to ensure that educational content is accurate, up-to-date, and evidence-based.

Supporting Local Initiatives

Cannabis cultivators can demonstrate their commitment to the well-being of their local communities by supporting local initiatives and contributing to community development. This can help build goodwill and establish the cultivator as a responsible and valued member of the community. Some ways to support local initiatives and contribute to the community's well-being include:

1. Donating a percentage of profits to local charities, nonprofits, or community organizations.

2. Sponsoring local events, sports teams, or community projects that align with the cultivator's values and mission.

3. Encouraging employees to volunteer their time and skills to support local causes and initiatives.

Promoting Responsible Cannabis Use and Addressing Stigmas

Cannabis cultivators can play a role in promoting responsible cannabis use and challenging stigmas and stereotypes associated with the industry. By modeling responsible practices and actively addressing misconceptions, cultivators can help foster a more positive and inclusive attitude toward cannabis within the community. Some strategies for promoting responsible cannabis use and addressing stigmas include:

Encouraging responsible consumption practices, such as starting with low doses, waiting for effects to onset before consuming more, and avoiding driving or operating heavy machinery while under the influence of cannabis.

Actively addressing stigmas and stereotypes associated with cannabis use, such as the "lazy stoner" stereotype, by highlighting the diverse range of people who use cannabis for various purposes, including medical, wellness, and recreational.

Collaborating with other cannabis industry stakeholders to develop and promote shared standards for responsible cannabis use, marketing, and advertising.

By engaging responsibly with their local communities and prioritizing education, cannabis cultivators can contribute to a more informed, inclusive, and responsible cannabis industry that benefits both consumers and the wider community.

The future of the cannabis industry depends on the commitment of cultivators to responsible cultivation practices and strict adherence to legal requirements. As the industry continues to grow and evolve, the role of cultivators in promoting sustainable practices, ensuring public safety, and fostering community acceptance becomes increasingly crucial. To support responsible and ethical cannabis production, ongoing education, collaboration, and advocacy are essential.

The Importance of Responsible Cultivation and Legal Compliance

Responsible cultivation and legal compliance are central to shaping a sustainable and ethical cannabis industry. By adhering to regulations and prioritizing environmentally friendly practices, cultivators can contribute to the industry's long-term success while minimizing negative impacts on the environment and public health. As the industry matures, cultivators who prioritize responsible practices and compliance will be better positioned to navigate evolving regulations and maintain the trust of consumers and stakeholders.

The Role of Cultivators

Cultivators play a pivotal role in promoting sustainable and eco-friendly cultivation practices that reduce the environmental impact of cannabis production. Cultivators can demonstrate their commitment to environmental stewardship and set a positive example for the industry by adopting water conservation, energy efficiency, integrated pest management, and waste reduction.

Similarly, ensuring public safety through proper storage, preventing unauthorized access, and prioritizing the well-being of vulnerable populations is a key responsibility of cultivators. By implementing robust security measures, child-resistant packaging, and educational initiatives, cultivators can protect their communities' and consumers' health and safety.

Fostering community acceptance is another crucial aspect of the cultivator's role. By engaging in open dialogue with neighbors and local stakeholders, supporting local initiatives, and actively addressing stigmas and misconceptions, cultivators can help to build trust and understanding in their communities.

The need for ongoing education, collaboration, and advocacy to support responsible and ethical cannabis production

The cannabis industry is a rapidly evolving landscape, making ongoing education, collaboration, and advocacy essential for cultivators seeking to promote responsible and ethical production. Staying informed about the latest research, best practices, and regulatory developments is crucial for cultivators to adapt and respond effectively to changing industry dynamics.

Collaboration with other stakeholders, such as researchers, healthcare professionals, regulators, and community organizations, can help cultivators to share knowledge, develop best practices, and address common challenges. Cultivators and other stakeholders can build a stronger, more resilient industry that benefits everyone involved by working together.

Finally, cultivators have a responsibility to advocate for responsible and ethical cannabis production, both within the industry and more broadly. By actively engaging in policy discussions, supporting sensible regulations, and promoting the benefits of responsible cultivation, cultivators can contribute to developing a sustainable and reputable cannabis industry that serves the needs of consumers, communities, and the environment.

In conclusion, the future of the cannabis industry rests on the commitment of cultivators to responsible cultivation, legal compliance, and active engagement with their communities. By prioritizing sustainable practices, public safety, and ongoing education, cultivators can help shape a more responsible and ethical cannabis industry that benefits everyone involved.

Conclusion

As we reach the end of our journey through the "Dope Cannabis Chronicles," it is clear that the world of cannabis is filled with endless possibilities. Throughout this book, we have explored the rich history, science, cultivation, consumption, and legal aspects of marijuana. We have aimed to equip you with the knowledge and understanding needed to navigate this dynamic landscape and make informed decisions about cannabis use.

Our exploration of the medicinal properties of cannabis has revealed its remarkable potential in alleviating symptoms and improving the quality of life for countless individuals. From chronic pain management to anxiety relief, from seizure control to nausea reduction, the therapeutic benefits of cannabinoids and terpenes are being increasingly recognized by medical professionals and researchers alike. As scientific studies continue to shed light on the intricacies of cannabis, we can expect even more breakthroughs in the field of medical marijuana.

On the recreational front, cannabis has emerged as a social and creative catalyst, fostering connection, relaxation, and inspiration. Whether it's enjoying a joint with friends, exploring new flavors through edibles, or immersing oneself in the artistic experience heightened by cannabis, the recreational use of marijuana has become a vibrant part of many people's lives. However, we must always approach cannabis use responsibly, being mindful of dosage, setting, and potential risks.

The cultivation section of this book has provided you with the necessary tools and insights to embark on your own growing journey. From selecting the right strain to understanding the intricacies of light, temperature, and nutrients, you now possess the knowledge to nurture and cultivate high-quality cannabis. Cultivation is a deeply rewarding endeavor, connecting us to the natural world and empowering us to create our own unique cannabis experiences.

We must always be mindful of the legal landscape surrounding cannabis. While progress has been made in many regions, it is essential to stay informed about the laws and regulations governing marijuana in your area. Compliance with local regulations ensures the sustainability of the cannabis industry and protects both individuals and communities.

In conclusion, the "Dope Cannabis Chronicles" is more than just a guidebook—it is an invitation to explore the potential of cannabis. It is a celebration of this incredible plant and its ability to heal, inspire, and connect us. By arming ourselves with knowledge, we can navigate the complexities of cannabis with confidence, embracing its myriad benefits while being responsible stewards of its use.

References

Andre, C. M., Hausman, J. F., & Guerriero, G. (2016). Cannabis sativa: The Plant of the Thousand and One Molecules. Frontiers in plant science, 7, 19. https://doi.org/10.3389/fpls.2016.00019

Grotenhermen, F., & Müller-Vahl, K. (Eds.). (2017). The Therapeutic Potential of Cannabis and Cannabinoids. Springer International Publishing.

Hazekamp, A. (2019). Cannabis: From Cultivar to Chemovar II—A Metabolomics Approach to Cannabis Classification. Cannabis and Cannabinoid Research, 4(2), 96–112. https://doi.org/10.1089/can.2018.0073

Hill, K. P. (2015). Medical Marijuana for Treatment of Chronic Pain and Other Medical and Psychiatric Problems: A Clinical Review. JAMA, 313(24), 2474–2483. https://doi.org/10.1001/jama.2015.6199

Kogan, N. M., & Mechoulam, R. (Eds.). (2020). Cannabinoids and the Brain. Springer International Publishing.

McPartland, J. M., & Russo, E. B. (Eds.). (2014). Cannabis and Cannabinoids: Pharmacology, Toxicology, and Therapeutic Potential. Routledge.

Mechoulam, R., Parker, L. A., & Gallily, R. (2002). Cannabidiol: An Overview of Some Pharmacological Aspects. Journal of Clinical Pharmacology, 42(S1), 11S–19S. https://doi.org/10.1177/0091270002238673

Pertwee, R. G. (2014). Handbook of Cannabis. Oxford University Press.

Russo, E. B. (2011). Taming THC: Potential Cannabis Synergy and Phytocannabinoid-terpenoid Entourage Effects. British Journal of Pharmacology, 163(7), 1344–

1364. https://doi.org/10.1111/j.1476-5381.2011.01238.x

Schaffer Library of Drug Policy. (n.d.). Marijuana Legalization and Regulation. Drug Policy Alliance. https://www.drugpolicy.org/issues/marijuana-legalization-and-regulation

Made in the USA
Thornton, CO
10/23/23 12:46:13